D1273963

UNIVERSITY THEOLOGY THEMES

Theological Anthropology

The Science of Man in His Relations to God

JOSEPH FICHTNER, O.S.C.

University of Notre Dame Press
1963

Nihil Obstat:

      Reverend William J. Hegge, O.S.C.
      Censor librorum

Imprimatur:

      ✠ Leo A. Pursley, D.D.
      Bishop of Fort Wayne-South Bend

UNIVERSITY OF NOTRE DAME PRESS

Library of Congress Catalog Card
Number: 63-15345

THEOLOGICAL ANTHROPOLOGY

INTRODUCTION

Man today is the object of much research and study. Every angle of his humanity has been scrutinized. Anthropology is only one of the many sciences which has dealt with the structure, development and history of man. The title itself has been adopted into the theological family in order to express that part of theology which focuses upon man and mankind. Our approach is theological because it begins with God and ultimately leads back to God. It is theological, too, because it springs from Sacred Scripture and the Christian thought of the ages. Theological anthropology, then, is the study of man from a divine viewpoint, or, to put it more precisely, it is one of the divine dimensions of human existence.[1]

Man has a double role in life: human and sacred, natural and supernatural. In his simplicity, God is able to see both the natural and supernatural dimensions of man, his totality and unity, at a single glance. He has no need of differentiating man into many elements as we are accustomed to do because of our rationalizing spirit. Unlike the Greek philosophers who had a prismatic view of man, the Hebrews, whose simple, pastoral life and thought

[1] I should like to acknowledge my great debt to three students of mine, Fraters Joseph Sullivan, John Igers, and Elroy Kelzenberg, who did the basic research for this essay and compiled much of the bibliography. I am grateful, too, to Father Erwin Rausch, O.S.C., for his kind and helpful reading and criticism of the manuscript.

are reflected in almost every biblical page, beheld the one reality that man is. They were theocentric even in their outlook upon man: he is made in the image and likeness of God. They had no systematized doctrine about him, neither an anthropology nor a psychology. Flesh, soul, breath of life, spirit were all gathered together into a human totality and unity. Man, according to the Hebrews, must be viewed synthetically as a physico-psychic organism, as a body-person.

It would be unfair to say that biblical and Christian anthropology are at odds with each other, that they have no complementarity. In the course of time, Greek philosophy emerged into biblical writings. On the other hand, to set up a Christian anthropology, medieval theology drew heavily upon Greek philosophy and fitted it with biblical and patristic thought. Within Christian anthropology the individual man is first taken apart and then pieced together in a composite unity. That is why in our study we are to see the individual man first as person, gifted with intelligence and freedom and weighted with responsibility, then as nature. His nature is to be a besouled body and an embodied soul, complete with an immortal spirit. Moreover, his nature is to be social, to feel his dependence upon his fellowmen. And so we are led to consider the communal man. In the total reflection of both biblical and Christian anthropology, we can see what manner of men we are.

We have already noted in this preview of our study that the first section will treat of man in his natural dimensions. The other section will describe the paradisaic situation in which man first found himself. That paradisaic situation was not merely natural but supernatural and preternatural. Man was created holy. When the First Adam or man lost his sanctity, it was recovered for himself and the rest of mankind by the Second Adam, the God-man. The Second Adam not only recouped the grace which originally deified and sanctified man in the garden of Paradise, but enriched man, individually and communally, far beyond his expectations. By the grace of Christ man has been turned into a new creature, a new man, a son of God. Man has not been able to regain all the original gifts, but he has been fortunate to retain intact his full humanity. He is no less a man after his fall into sin than he was before.

One set of gifts which the Second Adam did not recapture for mankind is the preternatural. We will study them under the heading of freedom. There were four freedoms in all — integrity or freedom from concupiscence, bodily immortality or freedom from death, impassibility or freedom from suffering, and knowledge or freedom from ignorance. At his debut on the earthly stage, man was endowed with these four freedoms so that he might commit himself entirely to God and enjoy the divine fellowship forever and his paradisaic state to the full. Since then, man, in spite of his hard effort and an abundance of grace, has never been fully integrated and entirely master of himself. Only in the heavenly paradise will he once again be free from concupiscence, death, suffering and ignorance.

Simply stated, the burden of theological anthropology is to inform us about the most captivating subject of all human interests, namely, man. Biblical history and the Christian heritage have proved that man is the apple of the divine eye. If God has shown so strong and large an interest in the man who is His image and likeness, then man ought to respond to the divine dimensions of human existence with a loving and grateful spirit.

THE TOTALITY AND UNITY OF MAN'S NATURAL DIMENSIONS

When we approach the subject of man, we inevitably begin to use the concepts and categories we have received from our Greek forefathers. The great contribution of the Greek philosophers to the progress of humanity was systematic, logical reasoning. According to Greek thought, man is a creature composed of body and soul, endowed with an intellect and a free will. Part of his make-up is matter, and matter to the Platonist is a substance, a sensible and measurable thing, essentially opposed to mind or spirit. Because matter is sensible, it is the source of evil and degradation in man. Plato placed little or no value in the sensible, seeing in it only a marred imitation of the world of ideas. That is how he carried his dualistic conception of the universe into his anthropology. There is at work in man an opposition of two co-principles, the One and the many. The body is the principle of division and evil; the soul the principle of unity and goodness. Human good lies in fleeing everything material and giving the soul-spirit free reign to contemplate the eternal ideas. On earth the unity of soul and body is a reproach. The soul is imprisoned, entombed in the body. One can question how far we Christians are still under this Platonist conception of man.

The Platonist dualism, however, is not characteristic of Aristotelianism and its counterpart, Thomism. Aristotle did not look upon matter as a thing but as a metaphysical aspect of reality. Matter as such does not exist; it is only a part of the basic structure of things. To Aristotle it was foolish to think that the soul alone does some things, the body others. It is the whole man, this besouled body, who acts. The body is not an independent substance, a thing existing by itself, but a metaphysical aspect of the one living reality, man. The body is man from one point of view. After death sets into the body, it disappears into a corpse, a heap of chemical elements.

Hebrew anthropology, which we can discern from the Bible, has no such dichotomy of body-soul. The Hebrew was prone to unify man. Man is not composed of body and soul (indeed, the Hebrew had no word for "body"), but entirely flesh, that is, a living, corporeal entity, *and* entirely soul, a living, dynamic source of activity. The Hebrew assumed the equivalent of the divine attitude toward creation: "God saw that all he had made was very good" (Gen. 1:31). With his eyes of faith, the Hebrew found the phenomenon of living corporeal reality to be beautiful and good because Yahweh had fashioned it, and he marvelled at the mystery of it all. His outlook was closer to that of the poet than to the philosopher. It did not dawn on him to search out the integral components of man, if that were possible to his mentality. Certainly he was a rational or thinking creature, but for him understanding was an act of the whole man, and not merely an act of the mind. The human heart was for him the seat of understanding and freedom. His view of life was diffused with faith, in which he saw God to be vital, forceful, faithful. Hebrew faith is spiritual understanding, a heartfelt commitment of the whole man to walk in the paths of the Lord. It energizes and moves him to listen and respond to the Spirit of the Lord within him.

What then is the flesh-spirit dichotomy we read about in the Bible, both in the Old Testament and in the New, particularly in the epistles of St. Paul?[2] Is it identical with the body-soul relationship of the Greeks? No, for the Hebrew flesh (*basar*) is the

---

2 See the chapter "Flesh and Spirit" in W. Grossouw's *The Spirituality of the New Testament,* trans. Martin Schoenberg, O.S.C. (St. Louis, Mo.: B. Herder Book Co., 1961).

whole man just as the soul (*nephesh*) is the whole man, so that there is little or no distinction between the two. The one stresses more the corporeal aspect, the other the dynamic aspect of the entire living man. The flesh-spirit dichotomy is somewhat akin to our distinction between the natural and supernatural. Faith taught the Hebrew that he was not only a creature but an image of God, and as such he was somewhat dualistic. He was meant to walk "not according to the flesh but according to the spirit" (Rom. 8:4). The flesh-spirit opposition that he felt caught him in between the natural and supernatural elements of his life. We who feel the same opposition can sympathize with the Hebrew position.

In the biblical perspective man is a living soul. His soul is not the disincarnate reality of Plato but the dynamic force of his being. His flesh is living to the extent that it draws its vital force from the soul. In fact, flesh without the soul is not flesh at all but dead matter, a corpse. The soul is even visible because it is in the world, feeding on the fruits of the earth, causing it to be flesh.

One aspect of Greek thought that suggests a comparison with the Hebrew is Plato's doctrine of participation. The sensible—what can be seen and felt — is an image of the eternal and unchangeable. Though it is a degraded image, it is designed to rouse us to a contemplation of the divine archetypes, the originals. This contemplation demands a leap beyond the sensible, beyond material things, if we are to achieve participation with the One. The Hebrew, too, believed strongly in the necessity of contemplation, but he differed much in his approach. His theocentric outlook on reality would never have permitted him to leap beyond the reality created by God. Creation was the image of its Maker, and the least of it contained hints of God revealing Himself. Like St. Francis of Assisi hundreds of years later, who saw God imaged in the bees, fish, flowers and fire, the Hebrew dared to contemplate and love things for the sake of the All-Holy in them. They were Someone to him. This is why we find in the Bible no dualism between contemplation and work. The Greek considered leisure a requisite for contemplation. He had to get away from it all if he was to discover God. The Hebrew was willing to mix contemplation with work. Because they were marks of his flesh, his care and worry and anxiety — not work — were opposed to contemplation.

We have seen so far, though only summarily, several basic characteristics and contrasts of Hebraic and Greek thought. Both together are our historical heritage, and both together have influenced, either consciously or unconsciously, our modern thinking and acting.

HEBREW ANTHROPOLOGY

Man Made to the Image of God

"God said, 'Let us make mankind in our image and likeness; and let them have dominion. . . .'

God created man in his image. In the image of God
he created him" (Gen. 1:26-27). Hebrew anthropology takes as its point of departure the revelation
that man mirrors the Almighty. As revealed fact, it
is the basis for theological anthropology: Man is
made somehow like God.

In this brief Hebraic vision of God and man we
see that when God speaks, His word is efficacious
and His command omnipotent. God is dynamic,
fruitful, mighty. He seems to deliberate over man,
setting man in a special relationship to Himself, but
once He has come to a conclusion He is ever true to
His word, faithful to His promise, willing to share
His dominion. Since there is no division in Him, His
acts never contradict His thoughts. And man is
patterned after God because he too thinks, speaks,
and acts. He has in himself three principal zones of
vitality: thoughts (heart), words (mouth), gestures
(hands and feet). Psalm 16:3-5 shows us all three
in juxtaposition. (Active participation in the liturgy
brings them all into play.) Yet man falls short of
the divine exemplar, for he is not always true to his
heart, not always faithful to his word, nor always upright in his actions: "God is not man that he should
speak falsely, nor human, that he should change his
mind. Is he one to speak and not act, to decree and
not fulfill?" (Num. 23:19).

In the original Hebrew the terms "image" and
"likeness" have a concrete meaning and are somewhat equivalent, although the latter term indicates

that there is no total similarity between the object and its resemblance. The likeness, taken in a concrete sense, is only an image approximating or resembling the object. Although all living things are somehow the image of God, because of the dynamic quality in them, man is a more perfect approximation. He bears the bulk of the dynamic life and activity among creatures: "He endows man with a strength of his own, and with power over all things else on earth" (Sir. 17:3).[3] Man alone is gifted with a heart of understanding and love similar to Yahweh's.

Anyone barely acquainted with the Bible knows that anthropomorphisms are central to its story. By anthropomorphisms we understand that the Word of God is couched in human thought and idiom. The question therefore arises whether there is a physical aspect to the image-idea in Genesis. Exegetes see only a minimum of the carnal notion in the human image of God. It occurs where man, the representative of God on earth, is pictured transmitting this image to his descendants (Gen. 5:1-3). The specific dimension or area of likeness is the *ruah* or spirit. Through his spirit man participates in the supernatural order (here we should recall the discussion of participation and contemplation), and is open to the life and work of the Spirit of God within him. Real encounter with God is possible to man in this

---

3 The whole passage, 17:1-17, is recommendable reading.

inner realm of his being, in the depths of his heart. If man resists the flesh and opens his heart to the Spirit, he will be led to understanding and love. If he should close himself and become hardhearted, he is stupid and foolish. He is to walk according to the spirit that is in him, namely, according to that likeness which at first is germinal and has to be cultivated and to grow. Man is called to be like God Who has a vital, active understanding and love. Because of that initial likeness, man must respond with all his thought and word and gesture — with his whole being. The call is an invocation to holiness. John the Apostle put pen to papyrus in order to transmit that call: "I write of what was from the beginning, what we have heard, what we have seen with our eyes, what we have looked upon and our hands have handled: of the Word of Life" (I Jn. 1:1-3).[4]

We have noted that man is the summit of all the goodness God has poured out in His creation. The image of God is the whole man, and in this image man encounters God. The image grows correspondingly closer the more freely and more responsibly the spirit of man responds to its Maker. Of all creatures on earth, man alone is allowed this holy rapport with Yahweh.

---

[4] For a lengthier treatment of this dynamic concept of the image of God, cf. Dom Bernard de Deradon, O.S.B., "L'homme á l'image de Dieu. Approche nouvelle à la lumière de l'anthropologie du sens commun," *Nouvelle Revue Théologique*, 80:7 (July-Aug., 1958), 683-695.

The Totality of Man

Flesh. The Israelite had no exact equivalent for the word "body" in the sense of the Greek term *soma.* To designate the corporeal aspect of a living being, the Israelite employed the word "flesh" (*basar; sarx* in the New Testament). Flesh corresponds to the combination of the Greek concepts of body and soul (*soma* and *psyche,* from which we derive the modern term "psychosomatic"). It refers to the whole being under the aspect of its corporality. Man experiences his concrete earthbound existence when "the flesh lusts against the spirit, and the spirit against the flesh" (Gal. 5:17). In other words, flesh is the index of his frailty and weakness, in contradistinction to the spirit which is his strength. Feeling within himself a tug of war, the Hebrew distinguished flesh and soul and spirit, but not to the extent of setting them in opposition. Man is entirely flesh — weak corporeal being, and at the same time entirely soul. All flesh is earthbound, in contrast with the Wholly Other Who fashioned him.

Soul. The term "soul" appears in Hebrew biblical literature 754 times, and with a variety of meanings. It simply denotes breath or respiration, the sign of life, and hence it can connote the throat or breathing canal. But primarily the soul is the principle of life, that which renders man a *living* being. The soul is not the disincarnate reality of the Greeks, but the whole man. "Then the Lord God formed man out of the dust of the ground and breathed into his nostrils

the breath of life, and man became a living being"
(Gen. 2:7). When the soul departs from a man, he
is no longer alive, and his flesh turns to dust. As a
vitalizing principle the soul is even identified at
times with pulsating blood. The soul is in a man's
blood, the seat of life (Lev. 17:11-12). Therefore,
no one is permitted to partake of any blood for
nourishment. When the blood oozes out of a man,
his soul dies. Later Old Testament references to the
soul's journey to Sheol do not prove that it is immortal. No book of the Old Testament mentions the
soul as a subsisting principle such as the Greek
psyche. The notion of immortality cropped up in
later Hebrew literature which fell under Greek influence. Wisdom 2:23 has the saying: "For God
formed man to be imperishable; the image of his
own nature he made him."

The soul is the seat of psychical phenomena and
religious sentiments. In this regard it is often paral-
leled with the spirit, but more closely linked to the
bodily organs such as the throat and blood. The
soul indicates the vital principle of human life,
which can die; the spirit the force and energy at the
core of human existence, which can never die.

Spirit. The spirit of a man is not strictly supernatural, but through it he encounters the Spirit of
God, which makes possible a life lived with God.
Specifically, it is breath or movement of air or wind,
suggesting the sensible atmosphere to be found in all

Hebrew thought. It implies something of the dynamic quality we noted above, a moving, active force within man. God put this spirit into man so that he might be open to the supernatural and docile to the entry of God in him. By means of it he is prepared for participation in the life of the divine Spirit.

Since it is often identified with the soul and the breath of life, it also assumes the functions of the latter two. It shares with the heart the role of the affective and intellective life. On the other hand, the spirit of man and the Spirit of God are not easily distinguishable in certain passages. The Hebrew came close to calling the spirit a supernatural element in man. The same parallel was carried over into the New Testament, where the authors writing in Greek play upon the idea of the spirit or *pneuma* of man and that of God. We catch a glimpse of this word-play in I Thessalonians 5:23: "And may the God of peace himself sanctify you completely, and may your spirit and soul and body be preserved sound. . . ."

Disregarding any precise point of reference, we may assert that "spirit" is a supernatural concept, proper to revelation. The biblical writers are definitely introducing an entirely new dimension into their anthropology. Later Greek thought developed a similar concept in the *theion ti,* something divine in man. The spirit enables man to enter into dialogue with God's spirit. Man has within himself this link with the Divine, lifting him up to a supernatural realm and permitting him a participation in the life of the Creator.

Breath of life. When Yahweh fashioned man, man was not yet alive, for he did not have vital breath. For the Hebrews, as for many of the ancient peoples, breath was not only the sign of life but also the vital force or principle of life. The living are they who breathe with their nostrils. Yahweh breathed into the nostrils of the first man the breath of life. Genesis 2:7 insinuates, by way of imagery, that the very first breath came from Yahweh Himself, that it was identical with His. Hebrew psychology shifted easily from breath to soul to spirit and interchanged them.

The Unity of Man

We have examined the three chief elements in the biblical concept of human nature: flesh, soul, spirit. Did the Hebrew think he was composed of two or three parts? No, a trichotomy or dichotomy was foreign to his thought. Such a conception would have seemed absurd to him with his concrete approach to reality. Man is not three, nor two, but one — one living reality. Human unity is portrayed by the Psalmist as he sings his praise of God: "Therefore my heart is glad and my soul rejoices, my body, too, abides in confidence" (Ps. 15:9). The dichotomy which appears between the flesh and

the spirit is not a dualism on the same plane of life,
but between the two orders of the natural and
supernatural. The opposition between the two orig-
inated with sin, and since the fall the flesh has
been in revolt. The flesh, that is, the whole man, is
no longer willing to serve the spirit which is ready
to walk in the path of the Lord. Man of himself is
not divided. Yet sin has dulled him to the call of
the Spirit and prevented his spirit from gaining full
and perfect mastery over the flesh.

The Psychic Functions of Man's Members

With his concrete, poetic, theocentric outlook on
life, the Hebrew did not distrust what is sensible in
man, nor see it as the source of sin. He agreed with
Yahweh that it was all very good. The Greeks would
have writhed in agony if someone had attributed
weeping to the soul or joy to the bowels, but the
Hebrew thought nothing of it. He just as easily related emotions, organic functions, and sensations to
the soul as to the organs, and conversely, thoughts
and sentiments to parts of the body. It is the whole
man who weeps, rejoices, despairs, thinks, and not
merely this or that part of him. The innermost feelings of his soul are mirrored in his eyes, expressed in
his gestures and bearing. The bowels, the reins, the
liver, the heart — all are essential organs of the
human body, and consequently of its psychic life as
well. If they are impaired, a man is not healthy and
has lost some of his vitality. For example, the

prophet Jeremiah exclaimed, "My breast! my breast! how I suffer! The walls of my heart!" (Jer. 4:19).

It is not surprising, then, to find the Hebrew relating the fundamental psychic functions proportionately to the central organs of the body. The center of the physical anatomy is likewise the center of spiritual activity. This is exemplified in the biblical idea of understanding, the primary act of man. Nothing but the most central part of the human being, the heart, could be the locus of this act. The heart is the seat of spiritual aspirations and knowledge, the home of the spirit, the fountain of freedom, even the abode of the soul itself, which occasionally was identified with blood. Thoughts arise from the heart, not the mind, and it is in the heart that truth lives. The heart believes, trusts, knows, loves, fears, and hopes. It is free to accept or reject the call of God, but its rejection of that call will make it hardhearted and subject to judgment. God knows the inner choice the heart has made and will judge accordingly.

Faith is the supreme act of human understanding. As understanding is basically dynamic and creative, so faith is a vital activity. Through faith man opens his heart and listens in freedom and responsibility to the call of the Spirit. "Faith then depends on hearing" (Rom. 10:17). Rather than stop there, it accepts the call and responds energetically. The call always invokes activity, and upon this activity faith thrives and grows. Faith is spiritual understanding, a living and creative dialogue between God and man. Faith, understanding, justification, life, love, all seem to converge into the whole man who is oriented toward God. To attribute faith and love to the heart was as natural for the Hebrew as placing grief in human eyes.

Up to this point of our study of theological anthropology, we have been shown the dynamic character of Hebrew thought. The beginning of their anthropology was with God, mysteriously present and involved in the life of his creation, man. He is the image of his Creator, the dynamic though sensible likeness of Yahweh. Deep mystery as he is, man crowns all creation, and alone is capable of responding on behalf of creation to his Maker. By the free and living faith of his heart, man can lay himself open to the Spirit and attain the goal God has set for him.

CHRISTIAN ANTHROPOLOGY

The Theology of the Individual Man

As we turn to a modern Christian approach to anthropology, we must draw upon the spiritual treasure of the Word of God. At the same time we must not neglect the profound wisdom of philosophy. Contemporary Christian anthropology is the outgrowth of two traditional fields of thought, the Hebrew and the Greek. Consequently, modern man regards himself as a body-soul unity. If he has the time and opportunity to analyze himself, he will discover phenomenological evidence of his unity. Let us personalize this part of our study, so that we can better evaluate and appreciate the advance of modern research.

We start with acts of reflection because they are essentially internal acts and not fabrications, that is, they do not pass over into the external world but remain within us. Hence they can instruct us about our individual make-up. In my act of reflection I see myself as a composite unity. I realize that I turn back upon myself; I am both subject and object, two poles of reality. Yet the two poles, objective and subjective, are both within me; I am aware not only of an ego, my *self,* but of the world itself within me. In a way, through reflection, I objectify myself. The world is part of me, an aspect of my existence, and to that extent a quasi-object.

Before taking up an analysis of the besouled body, let us look at a description of the body. The body is the entirety of my quasi-object. The body is not a possession of mine, as if I possessed it like a ball-point pen. It is I, partially yet not entirely. It would be more correct to say that I exist in my body, in the thoughts of my mind and the beating of my heart. I am the source of all my human processes, yet in such a way that they seem to happen to me, as if I had a twin-image of myself. I am aware of a subject and object in the very act of reflecting upon myself. I see myself as it were in the mirror of myself. I must conclude then that the whole realm of my being is neither totally objective nor totally subjective.

I experience in myself a strong contrast: as body I am a multiplicity in a unity, for the body is not altogether present to or immanent in me; as spiritual soul I am unique, incommunicable, simple, free, responsible, immanent. I cannot give myself away, nor can I cast the responsibility of my life and activity overboard. The contrast between body and soul is essential for the reason that my body can never replace my soul. The body can only be my embodiment, existing as a quasi-object for me. In every man additionally there is a spiritual ego which is his spiritual soul. Neither of the two can be withdrawn from the other.

Besouled Body

Whether we speak about the besouled body or the embodied soul, we refer to the whole man. The two terms are roughly synonymous with the biblical notion of flesh, which designates the whole man under a carnal aspect. Body and soul are the two principles of human composition. In a living human they are not to be thought of as distinct things, but rather as two aspects, irreducible but implied in each other. Even though the soul subsists after death, it is no longer soul (animating the body) but spirit. It is soul only in capacity and desire (in the desire of

once again complementing the body). We may say
phenomenologically that the body and soul dis-
appear together at death.

What is this embodiment or incarnation we all
experience? Through the body the human spirit is
situated in the world; through my body I become a
cosmopolitan. Embodiment is, therefore, a mode of
being-in-and-with-the-world. As soul I have an
orientation to the world; as body this orientation is
realized in me. My body is the medium by which I
am orientated toward my parents, children, em-
ployer, teacher, fellow-student, TV set, and so forth.
I must not disdain my embodiment, because it is the
handiwork of my Creator and my medium of unity
and solidarity with His creation. St. Thomas points
out that corporeal creatures should actually attract
us to God: "Creatures of themselves do not withdraw us from God, but lead us to him. . . . If, then,
they withdraw men from God, it is the fault of those
who use them foolishly." [5]

By means of the body I am surrounded with
space-time limitations. The body is my mode of
presence to the cosmos and of encounter with my
fellowmen. My body unifies me in the corporeal
elements of the world, and yet it is itself a weak uni-
fication, for it must feed and thrive upon the world
it inhabits. Because I am embodied, however, I can
enjoy solidarity with the bodily world round about

[5] *Summa Theologica*, I, q. 65, a. 1, ad 3.

me and gain support from it. I must live dynamically and holily through my body, and conversely other things live for me through my body.

Value of the body. The value of the body undoubtedly lies in its role of helpmate to the soul. First of all, it is a valuable means of action and achievement in our everyday life, not merely in our external way of acting, like tapping away at a typewriter, but in the most human acts of knowing and willing. Commenting on the union of the human soul and body, St. Thomas writes, "The soul is united to the body for the sake of intellection, which is its proper and principal operation. For this reason the body, being united to the rational soul, must be best disposed to serve the soul with respect to the things necessary for intellection." [6] So there is no actual thinking without the use of the body, for it is the totality of the man who thinks, and not simply his mind. This thought brings us back to our original consideration, that even in the primary act of reflection man needs his body. Without the quasi-objective world of my body, I (the subject) could not reflect upon myself (the object).

Secondly, the body is a vehicle of expression. By the act of speech, by clear, sonorous, forceful pronunciation we make ourselves understood. The vocal mode of expression is frequently the way in which boy meets girl. Speech conveys our thoughts,

---

[6] *De Anima,* a. VIII, 15, trans. John Patrick Rowan, *The Soul* (St. Louis, Mo.: B. Herder Book Co., 1949).

sentiments, ideals, the most intimate longings and
experiences of our life. Who does not become
aware of the mood of a friend simply by listening to
the way he speaks? Joy, anger, sorrow, love, all are
discernible in the tone, rhythm, and inflection given
to our words, "for out of the abundance of the heart
the mouth speaks" (Matt. 12:34). Moreover, the
eyes, the gestures, the bearing of a man are indica-
tive of his innermost self. If the old adage holds true,
that "the face is the mirror of the soul," then how
much more fully and significantly does the whole
body image and symbolize the personal mystery of
the soul. Through its lifelong union with the soul, the
body is gradually formed into its twin likeness,
moulded and stamped with the soul's history. The
body cannot easily play the soul false; it cannot
easily betray it with a lie.

Thirdly, the body is most valuable as a means of
personal communion, of intersubjectivity. The body
establishes my solidarity with the rest of mankind.
It brings me in contact with other personalities,
other egos. Our existential situation is such that we
can meet one another only through our embodiment.
Later we shall see that all of us have a solidarity
with our first parent in virtue of physical generation.
Liturgically too, we are able to join in worship because we are all incarnate. "For where two or three
are gathered together for my sake, there am I in the
midst of them" (Matt. 18:20). Every bodily gesture

and posture of ours at worship should manifest our longing and loving attitude toward God. If we are to enrich our environment, it must be with the means God has given us. We can encounter and benefit one another by and in every living bodily expression. Direct spiritual communication is not our lot upon earth.

Burden of the body. If our Christian anthropology asserts that the body has a value and dignity proper to its union with the soul, it does not deny at the same time that the body is burdensome. While the body is a means of action and self-realization in society, it is nonetheless an obstacle. To adopt for a moment the idiom coined by St. Francis of Assisi, we may say that Brother Ass has to serve us, but his obedience is exacted with much difficulty. How hard we have to strive to learn a new tongue, to train our fingers to a new task, to put our minds to an unpleasant problem, to escape sinful snares! The burden of the body which confronted St. Paul compelled him to cry out, "Unhappy man that I am! Who will deliver me from the body of this death?" (Rom. 7:24). Indeed, it seems as if the carnal self has a special resentment to all effort, so great is its tendency to pamper itself.

Although the body is a sign of the soul, it expresses the soul only in a veiled way. So often we try to no avail to make ourselves understood, to give life to our inner experiences and feelings, only

to find ourselves unknown or misunderstood. Our
body reveals nothing with absolute clarity. Almost
all corporeal signs prove vague and meaningless in
a moment of crisis. Worse yet, the body occasionally
proves an instrument of self-isolation instead of
communion, a wall hiding the soul and secluding it.
And if our relationship to mankind is so opaque, the
reason is that we are unable to know ourselves fully.
We noted earlier that the soul in its act of reflection
is not crystal clear to itself but must employ its
quasi-object, the body. Unfortunately the signs and
symbols my body affords me are not sufficient for
complete self-knowledge. I am both a presence to
myself and a mystery, a presence and an absence all
at once.

Unity and complexity. To call a man a besouled
body is to affirm the tension biblical writers saw between the flesh and the spirit. The body-soul composition is an opposition in the midst of an indissoluble
unity. Each element exists within the one whole
human unity in an irreducible relationship. The opposition springs from one and the other, from the
soul-principle of unity and centralization, and from
the body-principle of dispersion and multiplicity.
The substantial union and individuality of man do
not negate his conflict. At the same time that the
body is united to the soul, it is subject to the law of
matter inherent in it. Inasmuch as he possesses a
sensibility, able-bodied man is drawn to pleasure

which tears his flesh away from serving his spirit. "I chastise my body and bring it into subjection," says St. Paul (I Cor. 9:27). The two sources of his being tend to complement each other, and yet by their own internal law they split, so to say, his ego and complicate his life. The tension and anxiety he feels is a mark of this dichotomy. Yet man has an initial unity, a unity that is perfectible by effort, vigilance, and an ever ready response to grace.

What is the Christian explanation of the mystery of man's unity? The body is not meant to be loved and exalted for its own sake, though in saying so we must be wary of a Manichean attitude toward it. Of itself it is not a body at all, for dust it is and unto dust it will return (Gen. 3:19). The immense value and dignity of the body is due to the soul which quickens it and elevates it to be the image of God. The whole man is likened to his Creator, a body raised to the level of humanity by the infusion of the spirit God has created, a body accompanying and serving man in his journey back to God. Originally, man felt the body and soul tied together in complete harmony. Then sin established in man a tyrannical government subverting the whole order of unity.

Embodied Soul

The counterpart of the human body and its constant companion in life is the soul. The Fourth Lateran Council (1215) taught that man is composed of spirit and body.[7] Such is our Christian belief. But in view of past human history, one can raise the question whether there is a soul. At the time of Moses, for instance, it was not yet known within the Hebrew milieu that the human body is animated by a spiritual soul. It would be wrong for us to see in the insufflation of the breath of life into the first man, as reported in the book of Genesis, a direct and explicit reference to the infusion of the soul. But slight indications in the Old Testament text do show that the authors caught a glimpse of the spirituality of the soul, because their accounts describe man endowed with spiritual faculties. Our present-day Christian doctrine of animism holds that the human soul is actually one, but virtually threefold — vegetative, sensitive, and intellectual. This Christian belief was formulated by the Fourth Council of Constantinople in 869-870: "The Old and the New Testament both teach that man has one rational, intellectual soul. All the Fathers and the teachers of the Church emphatically affirm this same opinion in their theological discourses." [8]

The Thomistic teaching is that the soul is a component part of man. By component part we under-

---

[7] *The Sources of Catholic Dogma*, trans. Roy J. Deferrari from the thirtieth edition of Henry Denzinger's *Enchiridion Symbolorum* (St. Louis, Mo.: B. Herder Book Co., 1957), no. 428; see also no. 1655. Hereafter it will be quoted simply as Denzinger. The same *Enchiridion* was partially translated into *The Church Teaches* by the Jesuit Fathers of St. Mary's College, St. Mary's, Kansas, and published by Herder in 1955. Most of the translations here given were taken from the latter work.

[8] Denzinger, no. 338.

stand that it is the first principle of life, actualizing
and enlivening the body.[9] The soul is uniquely and
numerically the one substantial form of the body.
The Council of Vienne (1311-1312) condemned
Peter John Olivi's contrary opinion: "We condemn
as erroneous and opposed to Catholic truth every
doctrine and opinion that rashly asserts that the
substance of the rational, intellectual soul is not
truly and by its own nature the form of the human
body, or that casts doubt on this matter." [10]

Now that we have surveyed the Christian doctrine
concerning the soul, we can turn our attention to
the embodied soul of the unified man. The human
spirit united to the corporeal domain shares all the
advantages and is subject to all the limitations of
matter. As spiritual soul, however, man is subsistent
but open to help and support, independent but dependent. Because of the spirituality that is in him,
he is eminently a person. The personality of a man
is his I, his ego, his self. His personality prompts
him to be self-assertive, and cautions him not to be
self-centered and self-seeking. Christianity has always held the person in high respect, as is evidenced
by the traditional Thomistic teaching that "person
signifies what is most perfect in all nature — that is,
a subsistent individual of a rational nature."[11] From
this definition we can gather that corporeal beings

9 *Summa Theologica*, I, qq. 76-77.
10 Denzinger, no. 481.
11 *Summa Theologica*, I, q. 29, a. 3.

are individual, while spiritual beings are personal.
Individuality and personality are two aspects of the
human being, distinct but not separate. One and the
same reality is individual and personal, an individual by reason of that in him which derives from
matter, and a person by reason of that in him
which derives from spirit. Material individuality is
not in itself an evil; in fact, the Christian considers
it something good insofar as it is related to personality. Evil pokes its ugly head into the human
scene when preponderance is given to the individual, selfish aspect of being.

In spite of the conflicting tendencies of the individual nature and the personal spirit, the two are
co-principles of the one being, man. The personal
spirit actuates the individual nature and makes it
exist by informing, unifying, possessing, and devel-
oping it. The person is the determining ego, the "I"
at the source of every spiritual being. Rip out, if you
can, the personality of a man, and you have divested
him of his humanity. Man cannot be depersonalized
and still remain a member of human society, for it
is his personality which is irreplaceable and incommunicable.

From a Christian point of view, the spirit marks
the advent of a radically new dimension in the
cosmos. Through spirit the individual nature is
raised to the level of thought, freedom, responsibility. The person who identifies himself with this
spirit, introduces a decidedly new value into the

world. For at the root of his spirit lie the powers of knowing and loving God.

Intellectuality. One of the glories of man's personality is his ability to know. His intellect orientates him to truth and gives direction to his life. He can weigh the possible courses which lay open before him and determine for himself the goal of his existence. Every man has to face the question, what do I want to make out of my life? What meaning and value do I have?

The Christian has the possibility and opportunity of attaining to natural and supernatural knowledge, for he is open not only to created value but to Uncreated Good. Here we need to reflect on the biblical notion of spiritual understanding, which is synonymous with faith. Let us recall that the human spirit is defined by its relation to God; God has traced His image in the spirit, so that the spirit can find its way back to God by grace. Faith reveals to man, to his spirit, a supernatural world of truth in which he personally encounters God. God communicates to man by the grace of faith and love a living knowledge of Himself.

Freedom. Consistently throughout her history, and in the face of much attack upon her doctrine, the Church has affirmed the basic freedom of man. She has had to stem the attacks of the semi-Pelagians, Luther, Michel de Bay, Cornelis Jansen, Pasquier Quesnel, all of whom questioned or rejected the freedom of the rational soul after the fall of Adam. There is need in our contemporary life to reassert the power of free will, especially when some men in our society insist upon a certain determinism and make excuses for public crime.

The concept of freedom brings us to the heart of the human person. Freedom is not license or indifference to good and evil, but essentially the orientation of the whole man to goodness. His likeness to God orientates but does not necessitate man to goodness. The choice of this or that good demands the powers of understanding and free will. Freedom itself, however, is not a mere power or possession, but essentially the orientation of the whole man to goodness, to the power to do good. To be a man is to be free. As spirit, man is a subsistent and autonomous being, though his autonomy is not absolute or infallible. It is curbed on the one hand by the image of God within him and on the other by an understanding that is often vague about its object and a will that wavers between real and false good. And since it is the whole man who is orientated toward goodness, there is always the weakness of the flesh to cope with. Therefore, while orientated in one direction, he is capable of both good and evil.

Human freedom sheds light upon the world. By the use of his freedom, man can let reality live for him; he can assume the lower creation to himself — the earth with its natural resources, the heavens and all spatial bodies — and lift it up to the level of his own existence. In that sense man can create meaning for everything. The light of his freedom likewise reflects desire. Nothing is so boring for man as to accept the world about him matter-of-factly. He is obsessed with the desire to enrich and improve upon it, never fully satisfied with the reality he encounters outside and within himself. He will make himself anew. Being the self-creating entity that he is, he manifests by his light of freedom a spark of the divine creativity.

By his corporality man is caught up in the cosmos, but by his spirituality he is projected in another direction, one in which he finds himself transcendent over the world. He wants to free himself eventually from his solidarity with the cosmos and to attain to the goal of personal communion with God. This ultimate goal of man's being can be deduced from the fact that his desire for created values — wealth, power, prestige, for example — is never satiated. He always feels the desire for more lasting and complete happiness, which can only be fulfilled by the Wholly Other.

Responsibility. It is evident from the brief description of the human situation in Genesis that man was given a responsibility to himself, to his fellowman, and to the surrounding world. "Be fruitful and multiply; fill the earth and subdue it. Have dominion. . . . The Lord God took the man and placed him in the garden of Eden to till it and to keep it. 'It is not good that the man is alone; I will make him a helper like himself!' " (Gen. 1:28; 2:15,

18). And man was to cling to the wife given to him for companionship. Man first experienced responsibility when he was divinely commanded to eat one kind of fruit and not another in the garden. Man's moral consciousness inspires him to accept the reality of things as they are, to recognize that the reality facing him is for his use and not abuse. Creation challenges his initiative and creativity, if he is to better himself. Man is free to accept or reject the call of creation, but his response will not be morally indifferent. Whatever be his choice, he cannot neglect the fact that reality is itself a norm. Above all, when he meets with other persons, he must acknowledge and respect the value and dignity of the other man, just as he must respect his own. He cannot abuse the other man without simultaneously rejecting the meaning in life which the other has for him. Both together are orientated toward a sublime goal.

Creation is a gift and a duty. Man standing atop the world has no other moral alternative than to respond to the call of his nature and the nature of the world. As the king of creation, he must rule with all the force and dynamism given him and serve the creation from which he was fashioned. As the image of God, he has to be aware of his responsibility to both the corporeal and the supernatural reality of which he is a shareholder. His responsibility is primarily a religious concept, for God has spoken to him by the power of His Word, a Word that still resounds throughout nature and must evoke a response from the man to whom it is addressed. The world is man's means of dialogue with God.

The Theology of the Communal Man

All the while that we dwelt upon the theology of the individual man, his body-soul unity, we had the faint impression at least that the human person is not altogether self-contained. He co-exists; all of human life is intersubjective. He is a being in solidarity with the cosmos and with God. Corporeally he gathers up the world within himself, but spiritually he transcends it, raises it to the level of his own existence, and in turn is open and accessible to his Creator. Let us take the example of Abraham. Abraham, the semi-nomad sheik, the Chaldean, heard the call from Yahweh, "Leave your country, your kinsfolk and your father's house, for the land which I will show you; I will make a great nation of you" (Gen. 12:1-2). Abraham's corporeal and spiritual vocation contained the entire religious mission of the people of Israel. God chose not merely an individual but a people, and His call resounds throughout the Old Testament almost like a refrain: "Ever present in your midst, I will be your God, and you will be my people" (Lev. 26:12). People, nation, kingdom, assembly, remnant, Mystical Body — there in summary is the salvation history of the communal man, a history

beginning with the first man but renewed especially
in Abraham and recalled in many leaders thereafter.

Personality, that spiritual side of man, tends by
nature to communion, in virtue both of its value
and dignity and of its needs. The knowledge and
love, the freedom and responsibility, that enrich
and ennoble the personality require relationship
with other persons, because the personality is identical with a creative spirit that wants to communi-
cate whatever treasure it has. Likewise, personality
stands in need of dialogue with others because of
its deficiencies, derived not so much from itself as
from its material individuality. Man requires his
fellowman for food, clothing, recreation, government, politics, home, but much more for the acquisi-
tion of knowledge, love, and all other spiritual
prizes. Above all, if he is to be the epitome of the
cosmos, his spirit must be open to the transcendent
Creator.

St. Thomas has a balanced view of man's role
in society in respect of his material individuality
as well as of his spiritual personality. "Every individual person is compared to the whole community as part to whole."[12] In respect of his material
individuality man has to engage in and serve society
for sake of the common good, for example, by ac-
cepting a political position, risking his life in an
experiment, or laying down his life in time of a
just war. But in respect of his spiritual personality

12 *Summa Theologica*, II-II, q. 64, a. 2.

he is transcendent over society, and society must
bow to him, be just to him, and distribute its goods
equitably to him. "Man is not ordained to the body
politic, according to all that he is and has. . . . But
all that man is, and can, and has, must be referred
to God."[13] Education may be a fair example of a
boon which society must provide for its citizens,
in such a way too that they can refer every possession, every creative spirit to God.

Intersubjectivity or personal encounter makes
possible the knowledge and love of persons in human and divine society. The contact and experience
we have with other persons is an opening for us
to realize not only what they are but who they are.
The degree of presence with them or absence from
them will depend upon personal encounter. The in-
effable and inexpressible You can be understood
by contrast with my own I. Persons related to other
persons will combine knowledge and love into one
mutually enriching experience. Such an experience
is felt in the happy and lifelong union of husband
and wife. The individual is incomplete and one-
sided, while the person is complete and outgoing.
If we are to accept the totality and unity of man,
then we ought to concede that he calls for an I-Thou
relationship, man with man, and ultimately man
with God. God has elevated man above the rest of
creation and has bestowed on him a kindred spirit,

[13] *Ibid.*, I-II, q. 21, a. 4, ad 3.

free and responsible — the tremendous role of king and steward, with membership in the human community.

MAN IN A PARADISAIC SITUATION

Our portrait of man in his natural dimensions has shown us that the Hebrews, unlike the Greeks, expended no effort to analyze creation, to examine all its essential parts; but they did try to see God's creative activity in the functioning, growth, and development of the human reality. Christian anthropology, on the contrary, did evidence a spirit of analysis without forgetting that man is a body-soul unity. Taken together, Hebrew and Christian anthropology present man as a part of this world and the world a part of man. Man is a microcosm that reflects and reduplicates the macrocosm. He is the universe in miniature. Let us admit, nonetheless, that a definitive study of man will always be in the making. Creation itself is mysterious, and man and his relationship to God are doubly so. Man's role in creation is one of ever active and dynamic response and surrender, set as it is in a situation where man can enter into dialogue with a transcendent Person.

Totally authentic life is that which is orientated to the Absolute. It demands action in the service of God and of fellowmen. If the Hebrew and Christian view of life conspired to point toward a greater life to come, it sought this goal not in an escape from life, but rather in the development of the whole man.

Man, the glory of creation, is a dynamic unity bound up with nature but rising above it by means of his thought, freedom, and responsibility. To the scandal of the Greek world, God could endow man with the power to defy Him. Yet because man is made in His image and likeness, his freedom is likewise rooted in the responsibiltiy of responding, of entering the human self in dialogic relationship as a "Thou" to the absolute "I" of God. Only by transcending whatever is selfish and entering into fellowship with God will the self come into its own.

MAN'S ORIGINAL SUPERNATURAL DIMENSION
Sanctity of the First Adam

That man is meant for fellowship with God, that this is his goal in creation is established in the biblical account of the first man, Adam. The Genesis story reveals that man is to spend his life in the presence of God as the source and font of his being. Such is the situation which brings every man harmony and peace (we can speak of "everyman" in analogy with the "mankind" of Genesis 1:26). No theological anthropology which purports to study the full dimension of human existence would be complete if it failed to treat man's original supernatural dimension. After all, living in human history demands a realization of the entire space-time position. Time or *kairos* is of the essence for man. We accept *kairos* here in the sense of a definite moment of time, a fixed day having a fixed content without our having to know the actual date. A providential hour, a *kairos,* is authentic in its fullest dimensions only when salvation history is studied from *beginning* to end.

From the very beginning, the living God gratuitously took the initiative to put man in direct converse with Himself. Salvation consists in this encounter or personal fellowship with God called grace. The encounter is mutual, divine revelation and human response. Man cannot escape the duality which appears plainly in the relationship of nature and supernature. His two dimensions or areas of reality are distinct but not separate. The many complex relationships they involve have an application and interconnection with all the mysteries of the faith and the Christian life. The relationships are harmonizing as long as man is not torn between them by sinning. In viewing man in the totality and unity of his natural dimensions, we have only hinted at the new capacities and orientations which are given to man and which open for him new and permanent fields of dynamic activity.

The realm of supernature is a transforming and exalting quality: the entire scope of human existence is permeated with the divine and raised by it to a loftier plane. It is a new dimension wherein man lives and acts, a state engrafting the spiritual in the temporal. As parched lands soak up the summer rains, so is nature penetrated and soaked with the supernatural.

At the first moment that one steps into the human scene, he already enters into a supernatural atmosphere, for so has the loving will of God ordained. God has assigned a destiny which finds its ontological counterpart in man. His creative love pours out freely, elevating man to the position of a partner who himself is free to accept or reject the proffered love. If the divine love and life are accepted, they transform man intrinsically, vitalize, divinize him. The sublime divinization is so transcendent that only faith will accept it, and only a loving, grateful heart will experience the gratuity of it. None of it is his due.

What indications does the book of Genesis leave us of the supernatural situation of the first man? The elevation of Adam to a supernatural existence may be learned from the gifts which were so lavishly bestowed on him by the Creator. In fact, the bestowal of the gifts presupposes the special intervention of God. His plan is to uplift man; His acts are the expression of a creative love.

Adam and Even lived on familiar terms with Yahweh, Who, in the cool of the evening, walked in the garden (Gen. 3:8). They were made a little lower than the angels and crowned with glory and honor. They were never to grow hungry or weary upon the earth which the Lord filled with His bles-

---

sings (Ps. 8:6; Sir. 16:25-27). The above passages cast light on Genesis 1:26, "Let us make mankind in our image and likeness." Man is rooted in creation and at the same moment empowered to transcend it. John Milton, in the fourth book of his epic poem, *Paradise Lost,* was so fascinated by man's creation in the divine image that he cried out in admiration:

> . . . so lively shines
> In them divine resemblance, and such grace
> The hand that formed them on their shape
> hath poured!

Further evidence that our first parents were gifted with sanctifying grace and constituted in the supernatural order may be seen in the gift of integrity. "Both the man and his wife were naked, but they felt no shame" (Gen. 2:25). The fact that they had no feeling of shame, though they were naked, is again an indication of their innocence. The absence of shame would seem to be a concrete example characteristic of innocence, for shame is a defensive reaction against inordinate sexual desire. But the pre-fall nakedness may illustrate rather a condition of mutual trust and esteem than an absence of disorderly sexual drive. The primordial innocence suffered an irreparable setback when "the eyes of both were opened, and they realized that they were naked" (Gen. 3:7). The realization suggests a breach in the trust and the loss of an internal control by which the flesh was completely subordinate to the spirit.

There is no need of restricting ourselves to the Paradise story for confirmation of the Christian belief that the primitive state of man was free of sin, although the evidence is there to speak for itself. Ample evidence of a happy and innocent state appears elsewhere, particularly in the writings of the Church Fathers, who leave no room for doubting the fact. St. John Damascene portrays the first man in a high spiritual realm, wrapped in God's grace and wearing it as a glorious garment. One passage has this glowing description:

> And so God made man innocent, straightforward, virtuous, free from pain, free from care, ornamented with every virtue, and adorned with all good qualities. He made him a sort of miniature world within the larger one, another adoring angel, a compound, an eye-witness of the visible creation, an initiate of the invisible creation, lord of all things of earth, lorded over from on high, earthly and heavenly, passing and immortal, visible and spiritual, halfway between greatness and lowliness, at once spirit and flesh — spirit by grace and flesh by pride, the first that might endure and give glory to his Benefactor, and the second that he might suffer and by suffering be reminded and instructed not to glory in his greatness. He made him a living being to be governed here according to this present life, and then to be removed elsewhere, that is, to the world to come, and so to complete the mystery by becom-

ing divine through reversion to God — this, however, not by being transformed into the divine substance, but by participation in the divine illumination.[14]

In his crowning masterpiece, *The City of God,* which we will quote later, St. Augustine elaborates on the fact that man was created upright, and argues strongly for a paradisaic situation in which the lofty desires of the whole man are satisfied, both spiritual (in a life of grace) and physical (by the preternatural gifts).

Sanctity of the Second Adam

For a fuller understanding of the original supernatural condition of the first man, we have to consult the New Testament, especially the writings of St. Paul. They are replete with the idea that humanity has two heads, Adam and Christ, and that Christ is the Second Adam. The First Adam was only "a figure of him who was to come" (Rom. 5:14). Man's mirroring of the Divine Image is a scriptural theme underlying much of the Pauline theology. Man attains fulfillment in Christ, the New Adam, because the latter has renewed mankind in a state of justice and interior holiness which was lost by the First Adam. Paul visualizes the Genesis story continually growing in detail through a contrast of

14 St. John of Damascus (Book 2: "An Exact Exposition of the Orthodox Faith"), *The Fathers of the Church: Writings of St. John of Damascus,* trans. Frederick H. Chase, Jr. (New York: Fathers of the Church, Inc., 1958), p. 235.

the life bequeathed to us by the First Adam with that communicated to us by the Second. "So also it is written, 'The first man, Adam, became a living soul'; the last Adam became a life-giving spirit. But it is not the spiritual that comes first, but the physical, and then the spiritual. The first man was of the earth, earthy; the second man is from heaven, heavenly" (I Cor. 15:45-47).

According to the Pauline description, the antithesis existing between Adam and Christ is couched in terms of a contrast of sin-life and death-resurrection. "For since by a man came death, by a man also comes resurrection of the dead. For as in Adam all die, so in Christ all will be made to live" (I Cor. 15:21-22). The contrast aids our study of original man before the fall since Christ has restored supernatural life in abundance — restoring yet surpassing the life of grace which was the original gift.

Through Christ's death we have been reconciled to God the Father, and by His life we are saved. Before reconciliation was achieved by the one savior, Christ, it was necessary that sin should infect the whole race through the medium of the one man, Adam. We should beware of reversing the Pauline order of thought here. We are in the habit of thinking that redemption is universal because all men were poisoned with sin. The Apostle, however, wishes to emphasize that the new life of participation in Christ is prior in the divine intention. Sin spread to all men through the initiator, Adam, because the whole of the human race was to be affected by the life of Christ.

The grace of the Second Adam, although of the same kind as that of the First Adam, surpasses the original life of grace.

> For if by the offense of the one the many died, much more has the grace of God, and the gift in the grace of the one man Jesus Christ, abounded unto the many. Nor is the gift as it was in the case of one man's sin, for the judgment was from one man unto condemnation, but grace is from many offenses unto justification. For if by reason of the one man's offense death reigned through the one man, much more will they who receive the abundance of the grace and of the gift of justice reign in life through the one Jesus Christ (Rom. 5:15-17).

The contrast in the divine economy of salvation is from the one to the many — infectuous death; and from the many to the one — life in grace.

The biblical concept of the corporate personality illustrates the principle at stake here in a most striking manner. "As through one man sin entered into the world and through sin death . . . (so) the gift of grace of the one man, Jesus Christ, abounded unto the many" (Rom. 5:12, 15). In this context Paul shows the powerful influence one man can cast on a people. The point of comparison is developed precisely by means of the notion of solidarity in sin and solidarity in good. Corporate personality is a fluid concept often to be found in the

Bible, but it merits a bit of explanation because of its importance here. The concept is not altogether foreign to us today, even if we are unaccustomed to the term. The father of a family, for example, is held responsible for the actions of his children and they, in turn, may have to suffer the ignominy of having a wayward father. In a sense a single man can incorporate in himself an entire people; the community is crystallized in him. Just as all men were contained in the First Adam, so all men were present in and summed up in the Second Adam. The concept and reality of corporate personality cuts through time — past, present, future. Just as Adam actualized the human community and caught them up in his sinning, so did Christ sum up in Himself all who pertain to Him through His redemptive act. As head of a reborn humanity, Christ has, in principle, infused in all who are corporately united to Him a divine sonship. In the one man, Adam, there existed a corporate sinfulness, and in the other, Christ, a corporate sanctity. We are linked with Adam by a chain of physical generations, while in Christ we are directly orientated to God.

There is further corroboration in St. Paul's exhortations to the Colossians and Ephesians that the new supernatural life in Christ restored the original life of grace. Paul urges the Ephesians to be renewed in the spirit of their minds and thoughts and to "put on the new man, which has been created

according to God in justice and holiness of truth"
(Eph. 4:24). In nearly the same terms he tells the
Colossians to "strip off the old man with his deeds"
and to "put on the new, one that is being renewed
. . . 'according to the image of his Creator' " (Col.
3:9-10). Both passages allude to the Genesis account: grace revests the new man and reproduces
in him the original dimension in which he was
created to the image of God in justice and holiness.

We should be wary of identifying the old and new
man with Adam and Christ directly. The contrast
holds between one state and another. Human nature, vitiated by the primordial sin, is contrasted
with the new state of justification originating in
Christ. When we put on the new man, the heavenly
man, we are putting on Christ. Christ joined Jew
and Gentile that "he might create in himself one
new man, and make peace and reconcile both in one
body to God by the cross . . ." (Eph. 2:15-16).

If the Pauline antithesis of Adam and Christ is
to bear any fruit in our life, we must see its application in terms of continuity, development and fulfillment. By taking His flesh from the Virgin Mary,
the new Adam inserts himself into the continuity
of the human race, and at the same moment He en-
genders a new race created in justice and holiness.
The dimensions of the Incarnation itself begin to
broaden. The same creative Word Who fashioned
man from the virgin earth in the beginning of time
fashions Him anew within the Virgin's womb. The

relating of the conception of Christ to the creation of Adam inscribes the Incarnation within the continuity of a historical process.

The Christological communication of the life of grace is a development reuniting mankind to God in a most intimate manner. The Pauline antithesis lends itself to a double development. Adam and Christ are opposed to each other as the sinful man is opposed to the grace-filled man. Or the spiritual man has matured from the natural man. Both developments are valid, although one may receive more emphasis than the other. At any rate, in either perspective life through Christ consists of a participation in the divine nature.

Finally, life in Christ instils in us a sense of fulfillment, although the final meaning of human destiny will be revealed in God alone. "And this his good pleasure he purposed in him to be dispensed in the fullness of the times: to re-establish all things in Christ . . ." (Eph. 1:10). Whatever heavenly and earthly things exist, they are to be fully accomplished and restored in the new Adam. Here we have the precise meaning of recapitulation. Our corporate solidarity with Adam by virtue of our descendance is completely re-headed, re-established, and summed up under one heading, Christ. We are now corporately united in Him by reason of His position as head of a new humanity. Adamic Christology informs us that we have a new beginning which is a resumption of the first. Our life in the Second

Adam has been a renewal (II Cor. 4:16; Col. 3:10;
Eph. 4:23), a reconciliation (II Cor. 5:18; Rom.
5:11; Col. 1:20; Eph. 2:16), a re-creation (II Cor.
5:17), a redemption (Rom. 3:24; I Cor. 1:30;
Eph. 1:7), a regeneration (Tit. 3:5), in a word a
re-establishment (Eph. 1:10).

Even though Christ has restored the original gifts
of immortality and integrity by His exaltation and
glorification, still our possession of them has been
delayed until the last day. One reason for this is the
fact that the servant is not greater than the Master;
the members of the Body should undergo the same
experience which the Head has endured. Besides,
there is an obstacle to the full restoration inherent
in our fallen and redeemed nature. Our redemption
will have to be a gradual achievement. To restore
the gifts completely to us now would demand a
modification of our flesh-spirit nature. Historically
a complete restoration is impossible because it
would be tantamount to undoing Adam's free and
responsible decision. Only when Adam's causality
comes to an end will we come into the possession
of the original gifts.

Patristic Testimony

Irenaeus, the most important theologian of the
second century, borrowed the doctrine of recapitulation from St. Paul and made it the heart and soul
of his theology. He understood recapitulation to be
the taking up of all things existing since the begin-

ning of time and grouping them together in Christ. Christ has revitalized the original divine plan for salvation. Christ has become the second Adam, for in Him God has renewed, restored and reorganized all things.

Struggling with the Gnostics, who attempted to substitute knowledge for faith, Irenaeus is careful to emphasize a progressive view of sacred history, based on the unity of the divine plan. He observes that the divine plan has small beginnings and gradually unravels. The plan itself is divided into two great eons, the creation of Adam and the coming of Christ. When the First Adam and his posterity have proved themselves capable of possessing the Spirit of God (the sequel of events in the Old Testament witness to the proof), then the second phase of salvation history commences. Irenaeus reserves the term "recapitulation" for the second phase, and in so doing he gives a new twist to the Pauline teaching. One pregnant sentence epitomizes his thoughts:

> When he became incarnate and was made man, he recapitulated in himself the long history of man, summing up and giving us salvation in order that we might receive again in Christ Jesus what we had lost in Adam, that is, the image and likeness of God.[15]

15 *Adversus haereses,* 3, 18, 1, quoted by Johannes Quasten, *Patrology* (Westminster, Md.: Newman Press, 1960), vol. I, 296.

The doctrine of recapitulation — one can hardly miss the point of comparison — has evidence in it of the newly-coined term of corporate personality. Both suggest the idea of an easy passage of an individual to his community and vice versa.

Christ has re-enacted on a higher level all that has been done by Adam. The Incarnation is suddenly brought into focus by the application of recapitulation to creation. Christ has sanctified every aspect of human existence, including the historical, by becoming incarnate in order to save all men. The Incarnation is a reality and an event involving all mankind. Recapitulation, if it is to be authentic, must comprise all the dimensions of the first creation in order to restore and elevate it. To draw it out in full, one would have to resort to the Pauline conception of it in which he envisions the definitive realization of the recapitulation at the parousia.

Other Church Fathers have been equally concerned with the relationship between the First and Second Adam. Their lines of approach and the various viewpoints they take must each be set in its proper historical perspective. St. Cyril of Alexandria, locked in combat with the Nestorians over the true nature of the Incarnation, found it advantageous to stress the continuity of the Second Adam in the flesh of the first. The second elevated the first to a newness of life in holiness and incorruption. Christ makes all things anew in Himself and restores to us our condition as it existed at the start.[16]

With his usual theological acumen, St. Augustine perceives man standing midway between the fallen angelic world and fallen nature. Then he suggests that a twofold restoration has been effected by the Second Adam:

> For this reason the Apostle says: 'To re-establish all things in Christ that are in heaven and on earth, in him.' The things that are in heaven are re-established when that which was lost from among the angels is restored from the ranks of men; and the things that are on earth are re-established when those men who are predestined to eternal life are redeemed from their ancient corruption.[17]

In short, then, the Christ-Adam contrast attains its fullest stature in the Pauline and Patristic doctrine of recapitulation. The doctrine encapsulates the mystery of salvation history from the beginning to the end. In the Garden of Eden Yahweh blessed Adam with bountiful gifts and a share in His abundant life. But in the garden of Palestine Christ incarnated the fullness of the Godhead and recapitulated the fullness of man. Between God and man in Christ there exists a total solidarity.

16 St. Cyril of Alexandria, "Five Tomes Against Nestorius," "On the Incarnation Against Nestorius," and "Christ Is One," as contained in the book, *St. Cyril of Alexandria* (Oxford: James Parker and Co., 1881), pp. 8-9, 105, 121, 312.

17 St. Augustine, *Faith, Hope, and Charity*, in the Ancient Christian Writers Series (Westminster, Md.: Newman Bookshop, 1947), p. 63.

Ecclesiastical Pronouncements

St. Thomas has advanced two important reasons why the state of original justice required sanctifying grace. In the first place, original justice depended upon sanctifying grace as its root cause, just as human life is rooted in the human soul. Sanctifying grace established in man a resolute harmony with God. Secondly, the preternatural gifts were of such a nature that they integrated the first man. Consequently, sanctifying grace and the preternatural gifts orientated man toward God. The Thomistic position was historically unique in that it reacted against the contemporary opinion that man was not created in a supernatural existence. St. Thomas anticipated the action of the Council of Trent in declaring as a matter of divine, Catholic faith that our first parents were endowed with sanctifying grace and consequently placed in the supernatural order.[18]

The Church, ever careful to preserve the gratuity of original justice as well as the transcendency of grace, has been forced to condemn several errors which attacked the gratuity and transcendency, attributing to human nature powers beyond its capabilities.

The Second Council of Orange in 529 took speedy action against the semi-Pelagians in decreeing that "even if human nature remained in that

[18] Denzinger, no. 788.

integrity in which it was formed, it would in no way save itself without the help of its Creator."[19] For a while it seemed as if the attack upon the supernatural was kept in abeyance, but it started up again at the time of the Reformers. The Trentine definition did not settle the issue. Michel de Bay (c. 1513-1589) revived the Pelagian error, virtually denying the distinction between the natural and the supernatural. His proposition was condemned by St. Pius V in 1567: "The elevation of human nature to a participation of the divine nature was due to the integrity of man in his first state and for that reason should be called natural, not supernatural."[20] The same error cropped up in the writings of Pasquier Quesnel (1634-1719) and was condemned again in 1713 by Pope Clement XI. The error read: "The grace of Adam is a consequence of creation and was due to his whole and sound nature."[21] It is immediately apparent how de Bay and Quesnel wiped out the supernatural in one fell swoop. All of the conciliar texts quoted attest, if only by indirection, the gratuity and transcendency of the supernatural.

For us today who are accustomed and inured to pronouncements by the Church and canonized by ecclesiastical usage, there lurks a great tendency to take our rich heritage for granted. We forget that at one time or another in her tradition, the Church

19 Denzinger, no. 192.
20 Denzinger, nos. 1021, 1001-1009, 1079.
21 Denzinger, no. 1385.

was caught in a struggle for life or death against attacks upon her life and doctrine of grace. The Church has always maintained an orthodox equilibrium in her doctrine of grace, keeping the scale of doctrine from tipping to one or the other extreme, to defect or excess. Men have failed in their thinking about grace because they leaned toward an unhealthy naturalism (a defect) or pseudo-supernaturalism (an excess). In their naturalism they attributed too much power to free will, and in their pseudo-supernaturalism too much influence to grace. How the misconceptions arose is a matter of history.

Pelagianism was one of the very early heresies to declare all-out war on the doctrine of grace. The Pelagians were the Pharisees and Judaizers of their day. The Pharisees at the time of the gospel and the Judaizers in the apostolic age regarded justice as the fruit of their human efforts and pretended to merit by their works. It is this error which the Pelagians centuries later seized upon and attempted to revive. That pernicious doctrine, which can be glimpsed in every contemporary leaning toward naturalism, materialism and secularism, understood human nature as carrying within itself the seed of all humanly attainable good. The necessity of grace, even for our first parents, was rejected in favor of free will. By means of the ordinary powers given to his nature, man could avoid sin and attain heaven.

St. Augustine (430), who earned the title "Doctor of Grace" by his learned writings against the Pelagians, has helped us to come to a better understanding of the bountiful but mysterious life that God has imparted to souls. Pelagianism was formally condemned in 418 at the Council of Carthage, but vestiges of it remained in its sister doctrine, semi-Pelagianism, until the Council of Orange.

The history of man is a history of reaction. Ecclesiastical tradition not only bears witness to this fact, but has borne the brunt of each era's antithetical behavior. Over one thousand years elapsed before the many reactions to the Pelagian heresy solidified into a pseudo-supernaturalism. While the former error sinned by defect, in attributing all good to natural man, the latter sinned by excess, in denying that natural man is capable of any good or noble morality. Such was the doctrine of early Lutheranism.

Every heresy contains elements of truth, and the early Lutheran heresy was not without its positive elements. It held, and rightly so, that man left to himself cannot initiate any movement toward salvation; man is powerless to project himself into supernatural life with God. At this point Catholic teaching would have to agree. As a creature man is forced to act in accordance with his nature, and he must strive for a purpose inherent in his being. Supernatural life, and salvation in particular, so exceeds natural human power that no effort will produce actions conducive to a life with God. Consequently, salvation must be the work of God. But the Lutheran picture is not altogether clear. It is confused with naturalism in that Luther, Calvin and other Protestants subscribed to the Pelagian theory that Adam had only a natural innocence, for original justice was neither a free nor a surpassing gift. On the other hand, Lutherans have so exaggerated the effects of original sin that fallen man seemingly is incapable of doing any good at all. After the fall he was corrupt and remained so to the core of his being. Grace alone, without any naturally good support, is capable of saving man. Thus naturalism and pseudo-supernaturalism are combined into a single Lutheran misapprehension.

It is ironical to observe that the Epistle to the Romans, which was the Lutheran stumbling-block, contains a refutation in the balanced picture it presents. St. Paul admits a justification by faith — he who is just lives by faith — but he likewise takes note that the Spirit works in human activity. Elsewhere, St. Paul emphatically cautions Christians to "work out your salvation with fear and trembling; for it is God who of his good pleasure works in you both the will and the performance" (Phil. 2:12-13).

The doctrine of grace was to face yet another fight in the form of Jansenism. So subtle was Cornelis Jansen's theory that its effects stained the Church long after his death in 1638. Springing up in a period of general laxity in the Church, his

heresy claimed to have discovered the authentic
theology of grace in the writings of St. Augustine
which, it was felt, had unfortunately been misin-
terpreted. Like Lutheranism, Jansenism succumbed
to a false supernaturalism, conditioned by the view
that human nature was completely shattered by
Adam's fall. Unlike its near kin, Jansenism was the
result rather than the cause of misunderstanding
about grace. Since God has revealed Himself in the
past, it was thought that the Church should search
the wellsprings of her tradition for sake of the true
record. Such an investigation should reveal that
man does good or evil insofar as he is dominated
by either grace or concupiscence. Grace shackles
him to good, concupiscence to evil. All human impulses are sinful, even when they are irresistible.
God alone is wholly responsible for whatever good
there is in us, without any co-operation on our part.

We are sadly mistaken if we think that religious
errors are dead issues. The temptation to lean to
either extreme of the grace-nature polarity continually manifests itself, sometimes under new labels.
The Church has taken and always will take a middle path because she is well aware that the divinization of Adam and of Christians through grace is
wrapped in mystery and defies the probings of our
limited intellects. Mindful that religion is a divine-
human dialogue, the Church will always struggle
to preserve the real distinction between the natural

and the supernatural, which was so acutely manifest in man's paradisaic situation as contrasted with his fallen state.

Theological Investigations

Inquiry into the sanctity of the First Adam has led us, by way of comparison, to a consideration of the abundant life bestowed by the Second Adam. The latter has added an altogether new and Christian dimension to human existence. Basically and profoundly, He has overturned the evil wrought by man after the fall and has enabled the Christian to achieve a new destiny. We have observed, too, that the Church took up the question of the original sanctity of man in order to delineate more sharply her doctrine of grace, for grace began with Adam. Let us now turn our attention to a theological study of that first grace.

Whatever differences exist between the two creation accounts (Gen. 1-2:4; 2:4b-25), they both agree on the outstanding point that man is the chief work and glory of creation. God stoops benignly to create out of sheer love a creature enshrined in His divine image. But under what form did the divine condescension bestow the initial grace to man in his first existential state? What are some of the characteristics of that primordial grace?

The grace sanctifying Adam, though essentially the same as ours today, differed from ours according to the conditions of his existence. Adam could exercise a most wonderful control over his whole self. Flesh, soul, spirit were integrated in him and, with the help of the preternatural gifts, all things were subservient to his true self and orientated beyond himself to God. Adam was personally structured to live authentically. His life was truth, and no lie. Life itself, even as we know it nowadays, is a dialogic mode of existence which every creature must enter with its Creator. Adam lived that life to the full. He was open to the world, the beauties of creation, and responsive to the call of grace.

St. Thomas explains that man's elevation to the life of grace consisted in a triple subjection.

> The very rectitude of the primitive state, wherewith man was endowed by God, seems to require that . . . he was created in grace. For this rectitude consisted in his reason being subject to God, the lower powers to reason, and the body to the soul: and the first subjection was the cause of both the second and the third.[22]

His argument is that if this power of subjection was due to nature, it would have persisted after the fall. The triple subjection resulted in a profound harmony within man, so that the gift of grace exercised a more visible control over him. Visibly Adam was free from passibility, that is, mental and physical suffering; he had a bodily immortality and a domination over the natural world.

22 *Summa Theologica*, I, q. 95, a. 1.

Original grace exerted powers which now only lie dormant within it. It was a virginal grace, lacking a medicinal virtue, like an elixir which need not have had any healing qualities inasmuch as there was no damage from sin to repair. The grace was young, fresh, divinely vitalizing Adam and transforming his natural life.

The Adamic grace was creative. Adam was able to imprint upon the work God assigned to him — the care of creation — the characteristics of his divinization. He ordered all things to God; all of his work had a sacral effect. The dominion over the fish of the sea, the birds of the air, the cattle, over all the wild animals and every creature that crawls on the earth, the tilling and keeping of the garden of Eden — all of it came under the influence of his creative, vivifying work. Adam could face the truth and beauty of creation, settle himself in the divine milieu, and be instrumental in divinizing everything about him.

Because it was a gift of God the Father, original grace had the power of transforming Adam into an adopted son. A paternal gift draws the son closer to his father, and if the son gratefully accepts the gift, he endears himself all the more to his father. Granted that Adam was created and sanctified in the image of the Trinity,[23] the sanctifying grace of adoption came to him, not through the mediatorship of Christ, as does ours, but directly from the

23 *Ibid.*, I, q. 93, a. 5.

Father. His was an era of religious dialogue without intermediaries. Since the coming of Christ, religion has a mediary — He Who is the head of the new creation. For us, grace is the gift of a life-encounter with God the Father, through the Son, in the Holy Spirit, witnessed to by loving activity and orientated toward fulfillment at the parousia. Ever since the fall, grace has had a distinct Christological quality because it has been redemptive. Beginning with the fallen Adam and continuing throughout Old Testament history, grace was conferred in anticipation of the redemptive act of Christ, the Crucifixion. Salvation history is redemptive history revolving completely around the Second Adam.

One last point of contrast between original grace and redemptive grace is that the former was supernaturally invisible while the latter is supernaturally very much visible. Such a statement may seem strange at first sight. But let us reflect that Christ continues His redemptive work in the Church that He has established, and that the Church manifests the presence of His grace in the world. That is the reason why grace comes to us sacramentally, never in a purely interior fashion.

It is rather likely that original justice empowered Adam to evoke fervent acts of love of his Maker. St. Thomas says:

> We conclude, therefore, that in the state of innocence man's works were more meritorious than after sin was committed, if we consider the

degree of merit on the part of grace, which would have been more copious as meeting with no obstacle in human nature: and in like manner . . . because, as man would have had greater virtue, he would have performed greater works.[24]

Theologians have been divided in opinion over the minor question whether grace was conferred on Adam at the moment of his creation or was preceded by preparatory actual graces. Scripture is silent on this point. However, there seems to be more reason for holding that creation and the conferral of sanctifying grace were concomitant. Certainly in the case of children who are baptized in infancy no preparatory graces are given or needed. On the other hand, theologians object that the first grace should not have been granted to Adam without his consent, for he was created a free and responsible adult. Actual graces were needed preparatory to the infusion of sanctifying grace in him, as in the conversion of an adult. The Trentine Council did not show favor to either school of thought.

From the triple subjection traceable in the first man, it seems logical to infer that his life was embellished with supernatural virtue. The first subjection of his reason to God would have been directly dependent on the gift of sanctifying grace. Supernatural virtue was infused in him to subject his lower powers to reason. It remained for the gift of integrity to bring about the subservience of the body

24 *Ibid.*, I, q. 95, a. 4.

to the soul. In short, along with sanctifying grace Adam would have been infused with the theological and moral virtues inseparable from so eminent a gift. We can picture Adam, then, entirely open and accessible to God, exemplifying one, total subjection of a son to his Father. His natural life was thoroughly penetrated and imbued with the supernatural.

A word of caution is in order here against lavishing praise upon Adam for his moral and physical and intellectual prowess. The Fathers of the Church and medieval theologians were wont to postulate lofty powers in Adam because they assumed that he was created perfect in every respect. Sacred Scripture tells us very little about the qualities the first man possessed, and where biblical facts are lacking, arguments of fittingness are of little or no avail.

A whole theological history has fully developed the question of what is the constitutive element or essence of original justice. Did man's first innocence consist in the gift of sanctifying grace, the gift of integrity (*i.e.*, immunity from concupiscence), or both? And was the primal innocence, whatever be its quintessence, intended to be personal to Adam or common to the human race?

The writings of the influential Augustine are not particularly helpful in this connection. The Saint of Hippo thought that grace comprised all the gifts with which Adam had been endowed in his first state, that his privileges stemmed from the gratuitous dispensation of the divine life. In other words, the state of original justice *was* the state of grace. Are we then justified in stating that St. Augustine equated original justice with sanctifying grace? Some authors think so, basing themselves on books 13 and 14 of *The City of God,* but we should not hastily jump to this conclusion. We cut distinctions today in the tract on grace which Augustine never dreamt of. What we understand by sanctifying grace was beyond doubt in his mind the most precious and magnificent of the gifts granted to Adam. And yet Adam was the beneficiary of other gifts, immortality among them, which did not necessarily flow from the state of original justice.

Looking at the problem from the Augustinian viewpoint of original sin, we may be inclined to say that if Augustine identified concupiscence with original sin, he would logically have made original justice consist in the gift of integrity. Yet it seems that Augustine himself did not identify concupiscence with original sin; in his opinion concupiscence was its result rather than its cause. Concupiscence was a disorder, a derangement in man resulting from his pride of will, and, in pride of will rests the essence of original sin. Some of Augustine's followers, however, have defined original sin as concupiscence, and their opinion prevailed for many centuries.

St. Anselm of Canterbury (1109) was the first to expound the classic concept of original sin as

being the privation of original justice. Creditable as
it is, his description of original justice as "the rectitude of the will kept for its own sake" still leaves us
in doubt about his judgment of its exact nature.
Certainly he judges that the rectitude of the will
(which he calls "natural justice") is due to grace,
but it is only by reasoning from his texts that we
can link sanctifying grace with justice.

St. Thomas himself (1274) did not consider
sanctifying grace to be constitutive of original justice, nor its privation the essence of original sin. In
his estimation, original justice perfected the natural
man because it gave him peace and harmony from
within. Speaking technically, he would say that original justice was a preternatural rectitude of human
nature and altogether distinct from sanctifying grace.
As his thoughts on the question began to evolve and
crystallize, he saw a close interrelation between the
sanctifying grace in Adam and his preternatural
gifts. For its survival the former was dependent
upon the latter. The preternatural gifts did not add
to or change Adam's nature substantially, nor did
they raise him to the loftier level of the supernatural.
Rather they were a gift harmonizing and integrating
his nature, and as such they were a natural good.
The preternatural gifts laid the groundwork for the
fruitful and full reception of sanctifying grace,
which of itself elevates man to a supernatural life.
St. Thomas adopted this position because he was

thinking primarily of man and perhaps did not per-
ceive or relish our dichotomy between the natural
and supernatural orders.

Post-Tridentine Thomists, who undoubtedly were
influenced by the decisions of the council, favored
connecting the loss of sanctifying grace with original
sin and the spiritual death it brought to the soul.
They understood original justice to consist primarily
in sanctifying grace, and secondarily in the preternatural gifts. It is possible to trace in their opinion
the amalgamation of two trends of theological
thought, the Augustinian and Anselmian. They
equated original justice with neither sanctifying
grace nor the preternatural gifts, but with both.
They rightfully gave sanctifying grace prime importance, and in this way distinguished it sharply
from the preternatural gifts.

St. Thomas and his followers differed somewhat
in their interpretation of "nature." The master took
the term in the sense of specific nature, the nature
of man belonging to all of humanity, whereas his
followers had more in mind the concrete, individual,
existing nature. Perhaps it is because we have for-
gotten about the preternatural gifts, which are not
now available to us, that we deem a man just and
holy when he is in a stage of friendship with God,
that is, in the state of sanctifying grace. St. Thomas,
on the other hand, esteemed the first man because
of his natural endowment of harmony or rectitude.

Adam, the fountainhead of nature and grace, held within his grasp the power to transmit to his children the heritage of the gifts of sanctifying grace and integrity. We do not know precisely how he would have passed along that inheritance, or how God would have provided for its transmission. That teasing but highly speculative question is similar to the very practical one of the fate of unborn children, and it is not unlikely that the two questions hinge together. It would take us too far afield to enter into them here, but they do raise points of discussion.

No study of the First Adam can pretend to be complete, for our common father is shrouded in mystery. Mystery provokes our faith to continually seek understanding.

In Genesis Adam is pictured as an individual, and yet there is further reason to believe that the Genesis picture is of a corporate personality in whom all of us are caught up. In Adam we see the reflection of ourselves. He has the same dignity, the same potentialities, the same deficiences, and the same call to worship the Creator. Whether he be the moral, juridical, or physical head of the human race, one salient fact must be underscored — our solidarity in Adam. Adam summed up the community of mankind in his person, and we, the community of mankind, express and extend Adam the individual. The difficulty or impossibility we face is to draw an absolute distinction between him and us, for knowing Adam and ourselves as we do, we seem to waver between the two. The original Hebrew word "Adam," signifying "man," strikes a sympathetic chord in our hearts. For better or for worse, he was chosen by God to personify the people of God. The destiny of all mankind was his, but we may never forget that in the choice of his destiny he was our spokesman. We are his family, and whether we trace our lineage to him by physical generation or by divinely-appointed covenant, he is our common father, and together with him we form a corporate personality. Only when our solidarity in the Second Adam is complete in fact will we be able to overcome the sad effects of our first inheritance.

Thanks to the grace of the Second Adam, we have been supernaturally elevated to a divine milieu. Christ not only represents the entire human race but He *is* that race in that He consolidates in His person all men who belong to Him. That He redeems all men is the profession of our faith whenever we bring a child to the baptismal font to be reborn there. Christ stands at the head of a new creation, of the new people of God. The agonizing guilt-consciousness felt by the Old Testament people of God has been turned by the Second Adam into Christian joy, hope, triumph. We have a solidarity in the collective and cosmic triumph of Christ Who recapitulated all things in Himself. The new solidarity in Christ helps to divinize all our individual and common efforts. We and Adam converge into a single body, into Christ, so that we can gain the

victory of faith first implanted in Adam and then
transplanted by Christ. "It is he who gives to all
men life and breath and all things. And from one
man he has created the whole human race and made
them live all over the face of the earth . . . that they
should seek God, and perhaps grope after him and
find him, though he is not far enough from any one
of us. For in him we live and move and have our
being . . . we are the offspring of God" (Acts 17:25-
29).

MAN'S ORIGINAL PRETERNATURAL DIMENSION

Besides the two human dimensions already considered, the natural and supernatural, there is a
third, the preternatural. The name itself has no
familiar ring to it unless we are accustomed to hear
theological jargon. The first impression we have of
it is that it should stand categorically somewhere between the natural and supernatural, and our first
impression is correct. The preternatural gifts are
neither natural nor supernatural, but they so liberate
man that he can fully enter into fellowship with
God. They free him from the inner and outer deter-
minisms which hamper him from fulfilling his
destiny in life. Fallen man discovers sooner or later
that internal and external forces prey upon him and
keep him from loving God with his whole heart,
mind, and soul. The specters of death, suffering,
ignorance, concupiscence keep haunting him, tor-

turing his freedom, meddling with his responsibility to surrender himself completely to God's grace.

God prevented all the above factors from interfering with the supernatural life of the first man. Adam was set up in an ideal state; Eden was for him a bit of utopia, a golden age. John L. McKenzie, S.J., has paraphrased the Genesis description of that paradisaic situation:

> The condition of man at his creation is described vaguely, but the description is obviously intended to indicate a state of primitive peace and security. Man dominates the world of the animals; he lives in a garden, such as was attached to the palaces of the kings and wealthy in the ancient world. He is free from toil and mortality, for these do not appear until after his crime. Most significant of all is the intimacy with God which he enjoys; God walks in the garden in the cool of the evening as the lord of the manor strolls over his acres to refresh himself after the heat of the day. This simple intimacy was lost once and for all when man was expelled from the garden of God, the place where one finds God, so to speak, at home.[25]

Adam by the special grace of God was given the preternatural gifts of freedom from concupiscence, freedom from death, freedom from suffering, and freedom from ignorance. These four freedoms capacitated him to be thoroughly master of himself so

25 John L. McKenzie, S. J., *The Two-Edged Sword* (Milwaukee, Wis.: The Bruce Publishing Co., 1956), p. 93.

as to devote himself to his Creator unstintedly and with singlemindedness. Flesh, soul, spirit were harmonized in him. The peace reigning in Paradise as a result of man's domination over all creation was symbolic of the peace reigning within man himself. Unlike fallen man, Adam's lower powers were subordinate to his reason and his reason to the spirit. Once the total submission was disrupted by sin, disharmony and anarchy set into him, "for we know that all creation groans and travails in pain until now" (Rom. 8:22).

In order to gain a clearer idea of Adam's original condition, we will take up a more detailed examination of his preternatural gifts. We will review them in their relationship to man's supernatural life. Our intention is to show how each of them contributed to freeing man for the full pursuit of his vocation or call to divine friendship.

Freedom from Concupiscence

It has long been the teaching of the Catholic Church that our first parents in Paradise were free from concupiscence or, in positive terms, that they enjoyed the gift of integrity and were thereby free from internal conflict. Our teaching derives from biblical evidence and the testimony of the Church Fathers.

Chapter 2:25 of Genesis reads: "Both the man and his wife were naked, but they felt no shame." The text has generally been taken to mean that our first parents were innocent and at harmony with each other and God. The author of the text insinuates that if they had not been free of concupiscence, they would have felt shame. The sight of his naked partner would have caused an inordinate sexual desire in Adam, with a resultant feeling of shame, since shame is a defensive reaction against inordinate sexual desire. After Adam and Eve sinned, "the eyes of both were opened, and they realized that they were naked; so they sewed fig-leaves together and made themselves coverings" (Gen. 3:7). Here we are told about the occasion when the first man and his wife became conscious of their nakedness. Yahweh states the reason why they experienced the shameful and inordinate movements of concupiscence: "Who told you that you were naked? You have eaten then of the tree of which I commanded you not to eat" (Gen. 3:11). The contrast in our first parents' actions before and after sinning is a strong indication that they felt no concupiscence originally.

The true notion of concupiscence is not easy to arrive at, especially because through the centuries its meaning has been distorted or encrusted with private interpretations based on personal experience. What is concupiscence? The concept has borne a host of illegitimate children. The history of the notion has been stormy since the days of St. Paul. Catholic theology has insisted on a twofold viewpoint on the matter, which has not helped to clear the confusion.

In his Epistle to the Romans St. Paul calls concupiscence sin. "And do not yield your members to sin as weapons of iniquity. . . ." "But sin, having thus found an occasion, worked in me by means of the commandment all manner of lust . . ." (Rom. 6:13; 7:8). Much of the confusion arose over the texts because interpreters of Paul took his writing at its face value and came to conclusions later condemned by the Church. Paul's meaning was cleared up by the Church at the Council of Trent in 1546: "As for this concupiscence, which the Apostle sometimes calls sin, this holy council declares that the Catholic Church has never understood that it is called sin because there is, in the unregenerated, sin in the true and proper sense but only because it is from sin and inclines to sin." [26] Concupiscence is certainly latent in concrete personal sins and is a factor leading up to sin, but it does not constitute sin as such.

In the fourth century St. Augustine had to discuss concupiscence in his literary battles with the Pelagians, and his refutations closely connect sin and concupiscence. Thus in the minds of some of his readers sin and concupiscence came to be synonymous. With Augustine for his supporter, Luther in the sixteenth century taught that concupiscence is itself sinful. It is the corruption of human nature

26 Denzinger, no. 792.

brought about by the Adamic sin and is, therefore, the gangrenous core of original sin. Not long afterwards, Michel de Bay and Cornelis Jansen concocted similar opinions, only adding that concupiscence necessarily draws the will into sin unless grace intervenes.

Catholic writers and teachers have not been unaffected by the wrong opinions, although they have not gone so far as to assert that concupiscence is sin. It is one thing to maintain that concupiscence is the sensitive appetite in man tending toward evil in resistance to his good judgment and will power, and quite another to falsify concupiscence into something evil and sinful.

A proper quality of the sensitive human appetite is its characteristic of spontaneity. It is true that the appetite or desire reacts to a beautiful object or tasty morsel in such a way that it can anticipate and resist the free decision of the will. It is natural, for instance, that a man find feminine beauty and charm attractive. But this carefree tendency is premoral; it comes into play before judgment and consent. Good or evil are predicated of judgment and consent rather than of the spontaneity of a human desire. In fact, spontaneity marks our desire for food and drink, and if it did not we would be in sorry shape. It informs us, too, when we have had enough food and drink and also resists a weak or flabby will to over-eat or over-drink. The spontaneity of a sensitive appetite is unpredictable and may on occasion lead to sin, but as long as it is not determined to evil there appears no reason why it should be called evil.

Theology must recognize that concupiscence is characterized by spontaneity. Our first parents did not lack that spontaneity; they enjoyed the gift of integrity that gave them a total control over it. The gift was not a fitful possession which served them well only when they were tempted to evil. God did not make a fresh intervention into their psychological life every time they looked upon the forbidden fruit (assuming that they glanced at it more than once). We cannot imagine the integrity of Adam extending only to impulses which were outlawed by the moral code. With the gift of integrity for his continual possession, controlling the totality of his nature, Adam was gay and carefree. *bright*

Here we should make clear that the Adamic concupiscence (*i.e.*, spontaneity) was not a purely sensitive power. Man is a composite unity of body and soul, matter and spirit. Both are component parts and interdependent. When he acts, the whole man acts. Thus none of his acts are purely spiritual or purely sensitive. Even today when he meditates on Adam and Eve, he has need of his imagination. His intellect has a spontaneous urge for truth and his will for good. Should the intellect fall victim to falsehood under the guise of truth — as it might if it were persistently tempted against an article of faith — its fall, spontaneity and all, would be spiritual.

So often the temptations we experience are a spiritual and sensitive mixture.

The spiritual aspect of concupiscence has either not been given due attention, or else has been lost sight of altogether. The popular practice is to identify concupiscence with the lower passions or sensitive part of man, with the result that we think once the flesh is brought into subjection the fight is over. Who will deny that spiritual pride and spiritual lust are as pernicious as any fleshly disorder?

When St. Paul speaks about the flesh lusting against the spirit and the spirit against the flesh, he does not correlate the flesh with sensitive nature and spirit with the faculties of understanding and will. Flesh, in the Pauline sense, is the whole man under the domain of sin, that is, the thoughts, words, affections of a man who sets store by the things of earth.

Adam by the gift of integrity had complete control of the spontaneity of his being, sensitive and spiritual. We do not imply that no spontaneous impulse could arise in him. We simply maintain that he was a fully integrated man having complete control over his whole self, which did not render him immune to temptation and sin. Adam felt the same indeliberate and spontaneous instincts that we do. If we wish, we can label them concupiscence. But we should remember that the gift of integrity did not do away with them. In what respect then does our concupiscence differ from his? What experience of spontaneous desire do we have after the fall that Adam did not feel before the fall?

Whenever we act deliberately and freely, we have an objective in mind; we assume an attitude toward some object, for example, money, pleasure, prestige, virtue, holiness, a comfortable home. Our free will is a determining factor in our life and action, or else we would remain fixed, inert, static. Our will sways us one way or the other, and in so doing we adopt an attitude.

Whatever the attitude or posture, the human will is inclined to take total possession of a man and subject him to its choice:

> My free decision, issuing from my *auto*-determining faculty, inevitably seeks to shape and stamp my whole being, to affect me through and through, to seize on me and commit me in my entirety, to possess and master me as wholly as it can. When I choose I aim at throwing into that choice everything in me — even the blind spontaneous elements. I strive to make my choice articulate: to express, externalize, and 'advertise' me and all that I want to be and stand for. I endeavor to impregnate with my freely selected convictions even the darkest recesses of my being.[27]

The words "seek," "aim," "strive," "endeavor," in the above quotation describe the attempt of a person to dispose himself for action. In the present

27 P. J. Kenny, S. J., "The Problem of Concupiscence," *Theology Digest*, VIII, no. 3 (Autumn, 1960), 164.

order of reality, he never feels that he has full and exhaustive control of himself. Something always seems to escape his free and responsible judgment and will. The spontaneity in him continually offers an ounce of resistance and prevents him from measuring up to an ideal. An artist looks at his work and discovers that he has botched it. We all sense at times, no matter how attentive and careful we are, that our efforts are not as perfect as we should like them to be. A divisive and weak factor makes itself felt in us, and it springs from the duality of our flesh and spirit. Man, by his very definition of "rational animal," *i.e.*, a boundary line between two worlds, is a tragic figure. His assemblage of qualities, so complex and delicate a balance, can be had and sustained only by victories in constantly recurring conflicts.[28]

We have now come to the essence of concupiscence. The concupiscence from which Adam was free originally was that resistance, that inner division, that reluctant spontaneity which keeps us from wholehearted and free decision. Through the gift of integrity Adam was complete master of himself, fully in control, fully adjusted. Our concupiscence forestalls our complete gift of self, so that we cannot engage ourselves completely nor totally commit ourselves to a project. If we are freely determined to do a good work, our concupiscence prevents us

[28] Charles Journet, *The Meaning of Grace* (New York: P. J. Kenedy, 1960), p. 72.

from becoming wholly absorbed in it. If we have an evil intention, the resistance which is concupiscence will keep us from wholly committing ourselves to it. Unfortunately, man cannot give himself completely to good in this life, nor, fortunately, can he give himself completely to evil. Perhaps it would be better to speak of the gift of integrity as a freedom *for* than a freedom *from*: the gift freed Adam for a total commitment of self to God. Our failure to give to God all that we have and are betrays the concupiscence we have in us and the need for redemption.

It should be remembered finally that freedom from concupiscence was a gift to Adam, a gift he lost at the fall. In 1567, St. Pius V condemned Michel de Bay's error: "The integrity found in first creation was not a gratuitous elevation of human nature, but its natural condition." [29] By a special divine intervention in his behalf, Adam was freed from the resistance of concupiscence.

Freedom from Death

Hebrews and Christians alike have long believed that Adam and Eve would not have died had they not sinned. Our first parents had the gift of immortality; the Bible corroborates both the belief and the fact.

But the Hebrew, with his totalizing view of man, would not immediately conclude from a reading of Genesis that the first man and woman were immune

[29] Denzinger, nos. 1026, 1516.

from *physical* death. What his complete view was we shall see later. At any rate, several passages from Genesis contain indications that man was originally immune from death. After having placed man in a garden of delights, God commanded: "From every tree of the garden you may eat; but from the tree of the knowledge of good and evil you must not eat; for the day you eat of it, you must die." Later, when she is tempted by the serpent, Eve repeats Yahweh's instructions: " 'Of the fruit of the tree in the middle of the garden,' God said, 'you shall not eat, neither shall you touch it, lest you die' " (Gen. 2:16-17; 3:3). The sin of eating of the forbidden fruit brought punishment upon man: "In the sweat of your brow you shall eat bread, till you return to the ground, since out of it you were taken; for dust you are and unto dust you shall return." Human mortality stands in strong contrast with immortality: "And now perhaps he will put forth his hand and take also from the tree of life and eat, and live forever!" (Gen. 3:19; 3:22).

The tree of life was certainly a metaphorical expression for some means of preserving health and strength indefinitely. E. F. Sutcliffe, S.J., expressed the mind of many exegetes in writing that the tree of life "is probably to be conceived as having fruit of preternatural power capable of entirely restoring human energy and vitality and so of preserving the strength of youth. By its means, Adam and Eve, though mortal by nature, would have enjoyed the gift of immortality.[30] Similar to the fountain of youth or horn of plenty, the tree of life kept man from bodily dissolution. St. Thomas was of the opinion that the tree caused incorruption by warding off corruption for a while, and hence that Adam and Eve had need of its fruit more than once.

Conciliar pronouncements have reaffirmed the Catholic belief that Adam was immortal before the fall. The Sixteenth Council of Carthage in 418 rejected the Pelagian opinion that Adam was mortal and in any case would have died through natural necessity: "Whoever says that Adam, the first man, was created mortal so that, whether he sinned or not, he would have died a bodily death, that is, he would have departed from the body, not as a punishment for sin but by the necessity of his nature: let him be anathema." [31] The Council of Trent declared in 1546:

> If anyone does not profess that the first Adam immediately lost the justice and holiness in which he was constituted when he disobeyed the command of God in the Garden of Paradise; and that, through the offense of this sin, he incurred the wrath and the indignation of God, and consequently incurred the death with which God had previously threatened him . . . . let him be anathema.[32]

[30] E. F. Sutcliffe, S. J., "Genesis," in *A Catholic Commentary on Holy Scripture* (New York: Thomas Nelson and Sons, 1953), no. 143f.

[31] Denzinger, no. 101.

[32] Denzinger, no. 788.

The Trentine pronouncement is more explicit than the Carthaginian, which mentions only physical death, in pointing out the real primary effect of original sin, the loss of holiness and justice. Bodily death is only secondary and is more precisely a sign, manifestation, and seal of the other spiritual death. "Man's death is the demonstration of the fact that man has fallen away from God," writes Karl Rahner, S.J.[33] Jean Daniélou, S.J., sharply distinguishes between the two deaths: "Death is not the separation of soul and body. Death is the separation of man from God."[34] This in brief is the biblical meaning of death.

The Israelites, it must be understood, did not think in the same analytic categories as Western minds do today. They did not easily piece things apart and hold up each part for close examination or relate it to other parts. The whole thing, the whole man concrete and dynamic, was the center of their interest. Now the author of the Genesis story was an Israelite. Writing about the death Adam and Eve incurred by eating of the tree of good and evil, the author had not simply bodily death but total death in mind, a death of the spirit and the flesh. The Semites had no notion equivalent to our notion of merely physical death. Death for them was a single entity; it was total.

[33] Karl Rahner, S.J., *On the Theology of Death* (New York: Herder and Herder, 1961), p. 42.
[34] Jean Daniélou, S.J., "The Mystery of Life and Death," *Philosophy Today*, I, 2/4 (June, 1947), 118.

When God sent misfortune to the Israelites, they knew He was angry with them for their sins and that they were estranged from Him. Death and all evil they regarded as a sign of His anger and a prelude to final separation from Him. Job, for example, cried out in his misery, "But what is man's lot from God above, his inheritance from the Almighty on high? Is it not calamity for the unrighteous, and woe for evildoers?" (Job 31:3). Psalm 6, the first of the penitential psalms, reports the psalmist's affliction and his prayer for mercy and deliverance from death. If the psalmist had not resolved to rise from sin and leave the company of sinners, his state of estrangement would have meant death for him.

St. Paul, an Israelite himself, inherited the Hebrew outlook. His thoughts ran to only one death and that was the death resulting from estrangement from God by mortal sin. His thoughts show through his writings on death, especially in his consistent use of the one term, *thanatos*. The Epistle to the Romans plays upon the theme of death, but always under aspects of the same reality. Paul contrasts eternal death with eternal life in Chapter six, makes spiritual death follow immediately upon sin in Chapter seven, and in Chapter eight shows death to be the fruit of sin.

Within the broader framework of the Bible, then, lie the greater implications of Adam's sin and the real import of the death sentence issued against him and his progeny. The death at stake was more than a physical death for the reason that Adam did not die on that fateful day, but years later. What did happen on that day? The fact that the first man and wife were expelled from Paradise signifies that they lost the supernatural life of grace. Their physical death was the symbol of their estrangement from God.

The law of death reigned until the Second Adam came. He freely assumed our sinful nature and consequently faced physical death. Paul observes that Christ differs from all men in that "death shall no longer have dominion over him" because He never committed any sin. In His case physical death was not a seal or sign of separation from His Father. He put an end to the law of death, so that physical death no longer implies estrangement from God. In the New Testament and the Church Fathers Christian death is called a "falling asleep in the Lord," which connotes an eventual awakening. The meaning of death was so changed that Paul thought the victory and sting were taken out of it.

Is it entirely true that death entered into human life only because of sin, or is it a natural phenomenon and event too? Would death exist if Adam and Eve had not sinned? Michel de Bay's error was condemned by St. Pius V in 1567: "The immortality of the first man was not a gift of grace, but his natural condition."[35] Immunity from death, in

---

[35] Denzinger, no. 1078.

other words, was a gratuitous, unowed, preternatural gift from God. If freedom from death was a gift unowed to man, then death was and is natural, a phenomenon and event that should be. Yet man instinctively feels that it should not be, for he holds life dear. The conclusion to be drawn here is that every aspect of death is due to sin. Adam was preserved by the gift of immortality from the unpleasant, fearful, victimizing, dark aspect of death. His gift of immortality was opposed to the particular death we now know.

Had he remained faithful to God, Adam would not have experienced the tragic sense of passivity that death brings to all his children. We feel that it is an attack from without, an unwelcome guest, an encroachment upon our right to life. In the tragedy of death we are not only actors but victims of a sometimes painful and violent dissolution. For Adam death would have been the final achievement of his life, a culminating act in which he could express himself to his Creator freely and definitively. As a final episode it would have been an opportunity for him to climax his life with God, to encounter God face to face. In death Adam would have kept the integrity of his bodily constitution and brought his life to fulfillment and perfection. The gift of immortality would have disposed him to experience clearly a maturing from within and to make a total gift of self to God with a clear knowledge of his commitment.

Fallen man, on the other hand, cannot peer beyond the darkness of death. Death stealthily interferes with his freedom and thwarts his longing for peace and fellowship with God. Its elements of suffering, darkness, uncertainty, prevent man from disposing of himself utterly and lastingly. Death compels man to resort to the surrender of faith to God, to Whom belongs the final interpretation of human dying.

Freedom from Suffering

It has long been a point of Catholic tradition that in the Garden of Eden Adam led a life which was free from suffering of all kinds, that he was impassible or not susceptible to pain and anguish. The tradition rests mainly on the description of the garden of Eden in the book of Genesis: "The Lord God planted a garden in Eden, to the east, and he put there the man he had formed. The Lord God made to grow out of the ground all kinds of trees pleasant to the sight and good for food . . ." (Gen. 2:8-9).

The word "Eden" is derived from a Hebrew word signifying a place of delights and pleasures, a place where there was no sorrow or pain to disrupt human happiness. In the same line of thought St. Augustine wrote a description of Eden that leaves no room for suffering:

How, in fact, can anyone be called absolutely happy if he suffers from fear or sorrow?

On the other hand, what could have made our first parents either fearful or sorrowful, surrounded as they were by an abundance of good things, in a place where there was neither death nor ill health to be feared, where nothing was lacking that a well-ordered will could long for, and where nothing was present that could hinder man's material or mental happiness?

Now the point about Eden was that a man could live there as a man longs to live, but only so long as he longed to live as God willed him to live. Man in Eden lived in the enjoyment of God and he was good by a communication of the goodness of God. His life was free from want, and he was free to prolong his life as long as he chose. There were food and drink to keep away hunger and thirst and the tree of life to stave off death from senescence. There was not a sign or a seed of decay in man's body that could be a source of any physical pain. Not a sickness assailed him from within, and he feared no harm from without. His body was perfectly healthy and his soul completely at peace. And as in Eden itself there was never a day too hot or too cold, so in Adam who lived there, no fear or desire was ever so passionate as to worry his will. Of sorrows there was none at all and of joys none that was vain, although a perpetual joy that was genuine flowed from the presence of God, because God was loved with a "charity from a pure heart and a good conscience and faith unfeigned." Family affection was ensured by purity of love; body and mind worked in perfect accord; and there was an effortless observance of the law of God. Finally, neither leisure nor labor had ever to suffer from boredom or sloth.[36]

The foregoing description should not lead us to infer that Adam was not fully human, that the gift of impassibility eliminated in him all feelings and desires. Qualities like sensibility, sensuality, and sexuality belonged to him as to anyone else. The difference is that his qualities were free from sin. An Adamic society, without the fall, would have included human inequality — men and women who were unequal in intelligence, strength, sensitivity.

Is it possible to trace such a utopian description to ancient religions and mythologies? They all refer to some golden age when man lived without suffering and sorrow. That the golden age is so legendary may well attest that it has some foundation in truth and that the story contains real memories of origins. Or possibly it arose from some obscure instinctive belief that God in his infinite goodness could not have created man in his present condition.

Several ecclesiastical pronouncements are devoted to the question of impassibility and all point to an original state of felicity. The Council of Trent indicated that our present suffering and sorrow was not always the case: "If anyone does not profess . . . 'that it was the whole Adam, both body and soul, who was changed for the worse through the offense of this sin': let him be anathema." [37] We hesitate to

36 *The City of God*, bk. 14, chapter X, p. 26.
37 Denzinger, no. 788.

say, however, that original sin is the *sole* cause of suffering, because God may permit affliction to test and to train souls who are dear to Him. The gift of impassibility, as all the preternatural gifts, was unowed to Adam. Because it implied that immunity from affliction was natural to Adam, Pope Clement XI in 1713 condemned the statement by Pasquier Quesnel: "Never does God afflict the innocent; and afflictions always serve either to punish the sin or to purify the sinner." [38] And more recently, in his encyclical *Mystici Corporis* (1943), Pope Pius XII compared the extraordinary situation in which Adam found himself with the origin of the Church:

> Here it is pertinent to remark that, just as at the beginning of time God gave man's body the most extraordinary power to subject all creatures to himself and to increase and multiply and fill the earth, so at the beginning of the Christian era he gave the Church those means that were needed to overcome dangers without number and to fill not only the whole world but the realm of heaven as well. [39]

Here again a preternatural gift freed Adam to accept and respond fully to the call to divine fellowship. Violence, fear, sorrow, depression, pain, anxiety — everything that unduly disturbs man somewhat diminishes his freedom. In Adam such disturbances would have kept him from completely

[38] Denzinger, no. 1420.
[39] *Mystici Corporis*, trans. *The Mystical Body of Christ* (New York: The America Press, 1943), no. 28.

giving himself to God. Fallen man has only to look to his everyday life to recall how sorrow and suffering can hinder the total gift of self to God. A headache prevents him from paying full attention to his prayers; fear of danger upsets him; discouragement makes him an easy prey to temptation. The preternatural gift of impassibility in Adam checked these impediments and left the way clear for an intimate dialogue with his heavenly Father. Without impassibility, the only alternative left to fallen man is to accept his suffering in union with Christ on the cross.

Freedom from Ignorance

When the Lord God had formed out of the ground all the beasts of the field and the birds of the air, he brought them to the man to see what he would call them; for that which the man called each of them would be its name. The man named the cattle, all the birds of the air and all the beasts of the field . . . (Gen. 2:19-20).

If the inhabitants of Eden were to enjoy a close fellowship and union with God, they obviously had need for a certain freedom from ignorance and a certain level of intelligence. Adam was human and therefore endowed with an intellect; he was placed on the earth as an adult and therefore given some knowledge. But what was the quality and extent of his knowledge? Much that has been written on the subject wanders far from the skimpy data of revelation. We are almost given the impression that Adam was most knowledgeable, an expert, a superman. Patristic and medieval writers have read much into the given data and projected a developed culture onto the paradisaic situation.

St. Thomas himself was unduly influenced by his Aristotelian and Patristic forbears when he raised the question whether the first man knew all things and answered in the affirmative:

> Man named the animals. But names should be adapted to the nature of things. Therefore Adam knew the animals' natures; and in like manner he was possessed of the knowledge of all other things . . . as the first man was produced in his perfect state, as regards his body, for the work of generation, so also was his soul established in a perfect state to instruct and govern others. Now no one can instruct others unless he has knowledge, and so the first man was established by God in such a manner as to have knowledge of all those things for which man has a natural aptitude.[40]

This extract contains the reasons why St. Thomas and many other theologians have attributed to Adam a very high degree of knowledge: Adam was the first man, an adult father and instructor.

Since the Church has not committed herself about the quality or extent of Adam's knowledge, we are left free to form and hold a solid opinion. To picture his knowledge realistically, we must stick close

[40] *Summa Theologica*, I, q. 94, a. 3.

to the biblical account, which was written in a
primitive Hebrew milieu, and take into consideration pertinent archeological, anthropological, and
paleontological studies. Admittedly, the combination will not afford us much information, but it will
have the advantage of dispelling the imaginings we
have received from the past.

The Genesis story contains only vague hints of
Adam's knowledge: he was made to the image and
likeness of God; he was appointed to rule over creation; he was to till the earth, to name the animals;
he was not to eat of the tree of the knowledge of
good and evil.

Modern exegetes do not think that the naming of
animals reflects in Adam a knowledge of the nature
of things. Instead, it manifests the exercise of the
human intellect by which he was raised above the
rest of creation. Adam could well have designated
the animals by the external properties he saw in
them. To draw more out of the incident would seem
to be a case of reading too much into the story. M.
J. Lagrange, the famous Dominican exegete, has
commented on the problem as follows:

Adam named the animals. To do this it was
not necessary for him to know their intimate
natures; he could designate them by their visible
properties, just as we do today. It is clearly evident that one would be deceived in attributing
universal knowledge to Adam because of this
one passage, for the author only wanted to indi-

cate that man, at the beginning of his creation, was in full possession of an intelligence which alone constituted him the king of creation.[41]

The tree of knowledge of good and evil not only intrigued Adam and Eve as they stood in the garden, but its meaning — what it represented and what its relationship was to the knowledge of our first parents — has long intrigued biblical scholars. Up to now they have not been able to hit upon a satisfactory solution. Their consensus is that the knowledge of good and evil was an experimental knowledge which Yahweh did not wish to share with men. Perhaps He reserved it for Himself because it was the faculty of deciding personally what is good and what is evil. Our first parents in their state of creaturehood could lay no claim to such moral autonomy. To attempt such knowledge would have inverted the order of good and evil, which is the basis of every sin. They were not permitted to try everything once; they were to remain innocent as children "who as yet do not know good from bad" (Deut. 1:39). If we are prone to blame them for usurping a right not their own, then we ought also to strike our own breasts when we take a divine law into our own hands.

The most favorable exegetical position is that Adam's culture and knowledge were primitive

41 M. J. Lagrange, O.P., "L'Innocence et le Peché," *Revue Biblique* (1897), p. 348.

rather than highly developed. Paul Heinisch, the
Old Testament scholar, has written:

> . . . the knowledge of our first parents em-
> braced those things necessary and useful for them
> to fulfill the essential tasks entrusted to them by
> God, *e.g.,* to till the garden, to attain their super-
> natural end, to maintain love and increase it.
> It was the will of God that they should develop
> the faculties natural to body and soul through
> practice and experience, and in this manner to
> make progress.[42]

Modern archeology, anthropology, and paleon-
tology have discovered for us that the culture and
knowledge of man have developed and evolved
through the ages. According to the law of development, it is possible that Adam was possessed of a
very primitive type of culture with only a rudimen-
tary knowledge and understanding of his physical
environment. Raissa Maritain captured the outlook
of both modern biblical research and modern
science in the following remarks:

> Do not these simple commandments seem
> suited to a still very simple state of human in-
> telligence? They may well have been given by
> inner inspiration to a man who did not yet have
> words, for only later, in our opinion, would
> language be invented. . . . This virgin intellect
> was, as far as knowledge in the human mode
> goes, in an unimaginable state of simplicity and

---

[42] Paul Heinisch, *Theology of the Old Testament* (Collegeville,
Minn.: Liturgical Press, 1950), p. 165.

inexperience; yet its notions and ideas were rich with vast potentialities.[43]

Her remarks certainly do not conflict with the Church's teaching, which has been confined to the sanctity and integrity of the first man.

The law of development referred to above does not exclude the particular exception. Adam may well have had the perfect knowledge attributed to him by the Church Fathers and medieval theologians. What is known of the law of cultural development does not yet provide us with a full picture of human progress. Gaps still exist in the picture, particularly concerning the early years of the human race. Nevertheless, until the exception has been proved certain or more probable, the general law deserves priority.

It is equally difficult to produce any sure evidence about Adam's supernatural knowledge. It is an article of our faith that the first man was placed in the state of sanctifying grace or intimate fellowship with God. It seems reasonable to believe too that both his supernatural and preternatural gifts enabled him to submit himself, flesh and spirit, to God. Originally Adam was holy. If we envision him in a primitive state, we conclude that his was an unreflective experiential knowledge such as was common among primitive peoples. Since he predated the Old Testament, and since the author of Genesis

[43] Raissa Maritain, "Abraham and the Ascent of Conscience," in The Bridge, vol. I (New York: Pantheon, 1955), 42-43.

himself lived in a primitive society that had no
distinct knowledge of the mystery of the Trinity and
Incarnation, it is logical to infer that Adam's supernatural knowledge was very limited. Biblical and
scientific evidence converge upon the point that
Adam was a primitive man with primitive knowledge. Still it is too early to reach a definitive conclusion on the matter.

CONCLUSION

Our study of theological anthropology has taken
us through the three existential states of man. Once
upon a time man was in a state of innocence, and
that was the time that Yahweh constituted man the
priest of creation and all creation the temple of the
divine glory.

Man is an intermediary between the two worlds
of pure matter and pure spirit, a little world in himself. He is a nexus or point of contact between flesh
and spirit. As spirit he is intelligent, free, responsible. With original grace and integrity for his endow-
ments, the first man was able to symphonize his
whole self for the glory of God.

The rebellion man initiated against God was fol-
lowed by the loss of sanctifying grace and the preternatural gifts. The descendants of Adam can no
longer exercise complete control over the spontaneity of human nature but are subject now to the laws
of death, suffering, ignorance, concupiscence. All
creation has been in revolt and unrest in them.

The divine love for man is infinite. God Who is Love initiated a plan of redemption by which man could be saved from sin and be reinstated into fellowship with his Maker. He sent the Second Adam to recapitulate mankind and begin the last stage of salvation history. Christ has incorporated all of us into His life, death, Resurrection, and Ascension. All of our existential states are commemorated annually at the Easter Vigil in that glorious song of the *Exsultet*: "O truly necessary sin of Adam that Christ's death came to destroy! O blessed fault which gained us such and so great a Redeemer!" The paradisaic situation has not been lost forever; it has been regained for us in a heavenly paradise.

This study of theological anthropology should have taught us the divine-like dignity and value of man. At the end of it each of us can soliloquize as Hamlet did: "What a piece of work is a man! how noble in reason! how infinite in faculty! in form and moving how express and admirable! in action how like an angel! in apprehension how like a god! the beauty of the world! the paragon of animals!"

READING LIST

Books

Bouyer, Louis. *The Meaning of Sacred Scripture*. Notre Dame, Ind.: University of Notre Dame Press, 1958

———. *The Spirit and Forms of Protestantism*. Westminster, Md.: Newman Press, 1956.

Cozens, M. L. *A Handbook of Heresies*. New York: Sheed and Ward, 1947.

Daniélou, Jean. *Christ and Us*. New York: Sheed and Ward, 1961.

———. *From Shadows to Reality*. Westminster, Md.: Newman Press, 1960.

Gilson, Etiénne. *Introduction à l'étude de Saint Augustin*. Paris: Librairie Philosophique J. Vrin, 1931.

Häring, Bernard. *The Law of Christ*. Westminster, Md.: Newman Press, 1961.

Henry, A. M. (ed.). *God and His Creatures*. Chicago: Fides Press, 1955.

Luijpen, Wilhelm. *Existential Phenomenology*. Pittsburgh, Pa.: Duquesne University Press, 1960.

Marcel, Gabriel. *The Mystery of Being*. 2 vols. Chicago: Henry Regnery Co., 1951.

Maritain, Jacques. *The Person and the Common Good*. London: Geoffrey Bles, 1948.

———. *Three Reformers: Luther, Descartes, Rousseau*. New York: Charles Scribner's Sons, 1940.

Mouroux, Jean. *The Meaning of Man*. New York: Image Books, 1961.

Rahner, Karl. *Theological Investigations*, vol. I. Baltimore, Md.: Helicon Press, 1961.

Scheeben, Matthias Joseph. *Nature and Grace*. St. Louis, Mo.: B. Herder Book Co., 1954.

Schillebeeckx, E. H. *Le Christ Sacrément de la Rencontre de Dieu*. Paris: Editions du Cerf, 1960.

Tresmontant, Claude. *A Study of Hebrew Thought*. New York: Desclée Co., 1960.

Urs von Balthasar, Hans. *Science, Religion and Christianity*. London: Burns and Oates, 1958.

Van Imschoot, P. *Théologie de L'Ancien Testament*. 2 vols. Paris: Desclée Co., 1954, 1956.

Vawter, Bruce. *A Path Through Genesis*. New York: Sheed and Ward, 1956.

ARTICLES

Asselin, D. T. "The Notion of Dominion in Genesis 1-3," *The Catholic Biblical Quarterly*, XV (1954), 277-294.

Barrosse, Thomas. "Death and Sin in St. Paul's Epistle to the Romans," *The Catholic Biblical Quarterly*, XV (1953), 438-439.

De Letter, P. "If Adam Had Not Sinned . . .," *Irish Theological Quarterly*, XXVIII, no. 2 (April, 1961), 115-125.

———. "The Reparation of Our Fallen Nature," *The Thomist*, XXIII, no. 4 (Oct., 1960), 564-583.

———. "Original Sin, Privation of Original Justice," *The Thomist*, XVII (Oct., 1954), 469-509.

Gleason, R. W. "Toward a Theology of Death," *Thought*, XXXII, no. 124 (Spring, 1957), 39-68.

Lauer, Quentin. "The Genius of Biblical Thought," in *The Bridge*, vol. II. New York: Pantheon Books Inc., 1956, 191-211.

McGrath, Oswin. "St. Thomas' Theory of Original Sin," *The Thomist*, XVI, no. 2 (April, 1953), 161 ff.

Reilly, C. "Adam and Primitive Man," *Irish Theological Quarterly*, XXVII, no. 4 (Oct., 1959), 331-345.

Staffner, Hans. "St. Augustine on Original Sin," *Theology Digest*, IX, no. 2 (Spring, 1961), 115-120.

Vollert, C. "Saint Thomas on Sanctifying Grace and Original Justice," *Theological Studies*, II, no. 3 (Sept., 1941), 367-387.

———. "Two Senses of Original Justice in Medieval Theology," *Theological Studies*, V (1944), 3-23.